THE
OUTSIDER'S GUIDE
to
SPRING CEREALS

1995 Edition

Outsiders Guide

THE
OUTSIDER'S GUIDE
to
SPRING CEREALS

1995 Edition

THE
OUTSIDER'S GUIDE
to
CROP PRODUCTION

1995 Edition

PUBLISHER

ACKNOWLEDGEMENTS

The Publisher is grateful for the cooperation provided by all those sources listed under tables or charts within this publication.

In particular acknowledgement is given to:

Peter Hutchinson (The Agricultural Budgeting & Costing Book, Editions 38 and 39,1994) which has provided data used in most gross margin tables.

Mary Abbot who compiles 'Insider Track' for providing much data used in tables and charts.

John Nix (Farm Management Pocket Book) for data used in fixed costs and field work rates data.

OUTSIDERS GUIDE TO CROP PRODUCTION 1995

Printed and bound by Da Costa Print, 35 - 37 Queensland Road, London N7 AH

OUTSIDER'S GUIDE TO CROP PRODUCTION

THE OUTSIDER'S GUIDE SERIES

This is just one of the books in the Outsider's Guide series. There are three currently available. These are the Outsider's Guide to Crops, Animals and Horticulture.

The Outsider's Guides were specifically created to meet the need for concise, up-to-date information as a hand book. The Outsider's Guide provides key information about an enterprise in an easy to use and readily accessible layout.

This series is for all those who have not been involved in agriculture on a day to day basis but are about to be, or those that occasionally need to understand the nature of the business of farmers and growers.

Many people from many professions are using the Outsider's Guide. These are bank staff, accountants, agricultural students, journalists, loss adjusters, sales staff of agricultural suppliers, tax inspectors and advisory staff.

The series is an essential reference for every professional providing services to farmers and growers in the United kingdom.

THE OUTSIDER'S GUIDE TO CROP PRODUCTION

The Outsider's Guide to Crop Production provides a concise guide to the main features of the seven main arable crop enterprises on British Farms today. Each crop enterprise is presented following the same easy-to-follow layout in eight sections.

You are introduced to the enterprise through an overview of production in the UK and the European Union. Interesting comparisons between member states are made and the main trends are illustrated. A novel benefit of this section is the list of key questions and performance indicators provided which enable you to assess a farmer's success.

Marketing is the key to any successful business and the factors which influence this are considered in this section, from product quality to market outlets and prices.

After setting the scene in this way, the Outsider's Guide then takes you logically through the husbandry of each crop illustrating and explaining the nature of the decisions that the farmer has to make.

Naturally enough, this starts with a look at the best environment for the crop and production system appropriate to the farm's location and intended market. Growth stages are provided as these invariably dictate the timing of so many field activities. Crop nutrition, health, and harvesting of crops are summarised in the subsequent three sections, before all these elements are brought together in 'Performance'. This will provide you with a summary of how a crop enterprise performs financially, and provides you with an indication of margins and overhead (investment) costs.

The Outsider's Guide to Crop Production concludes with two sections. These are a resume of the Common Agricultural Policy support for each crop enterprise and finally some useful references, contacts and a glossary of terms used in crop production.

OUTSIDER'S GUIDE TO CROP PRODUCTION

CONTENTS

CONTENTS

CONTENTS

OUTSIDER'S GUIDE

WORLD PRODUCTION

Spring cereals are less productive than the winter alternative in temperate zones. Continental zones generally produce winter conditions too severe for survival. Hence the main spring cereal producers are as follows:

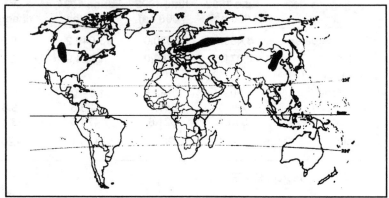

EUROPEAN COMMUNITY

Winter cereals predominate in Western Europe. Spring cereals play a subsidiary role on poorer land and as a rotation crop (see 🌳).

UK Spring Cereal Production 1994

Wheat	12.9 mt
Spring Barley	**2.3 mt**
Winter Barley	3.7mt
Barley Total	6.0mt
All cereals	**19.5 million t**

PRODUCTION TRENDS

The importance of spring crops has diminished over the past 25 years owing mainly to technological advances. Chemical pest control has allowed winter cereals to express more of their yield potential and encouraged plant breeders to concentrate their efforts mainly towards winter cereal varieties. The yield gap between winter and spring cereals now reaches 40% or more in good conditions.

PRODUCTION

UK PRODUCTION

Cereal Crop 1994

| | June Census results for UK | | | |
	June 1992 ('000 ha)	June 1993 ('000 ha)	June 1994 ('000ha)	% change
Total cereals	3,489.0	3,030.0	3,049.2	+0.6
Wheat	2,071.6	1,760.0	1,824.9	+3.8
Barley :				
Total	1,309.4	1,163.5	1,098.3	-5.7
Winter	784.0	641.7	623.8	-3.8
Spring	513.4	521.8	474.5	-8.1
Oats	104.4	90.1	110.1	+20

Source: MAFF

Most Spring wheats are actually Autumn drilled often after late harvested potatoes or sugar beet. Autumn drilling a Spring wheat variety increases the yield potential but there is a risk of winter kill in severe winters.

Spring barley is easily the most important of the spring cereals, grown particularly for the malting market.

The UK winter oat acreage for 1994 estimated at 60% compared to a spring crop of 40%.

WHY GROW SPRING CEREALS?

i   Better price -more likely to command **quality premium** (malting- spring barley, milling spirng wheat).

ii   **Costs less to grow** and spreads seasonal workload.

iii   Have **fewer weed, pest and disease** problems than winter crops.

iv   **Better quality straw** for animal feed. (Spring oats and Spring barley) v **Other benefits:** Straight forward gross margin comparison with other crops must take account of long term benefits (e.g. **reduced inputs**), and the potential **reduction in fixed costs** associated with a decreased autumn workload.

vi **Variable costs** are less for spring sown cereals. This has implications for cash flow and interest charges on working capital.

vii **Arable silage.** Spring barley can give a valuable yield of fodder dry matter and when grown with peas provides a nitrogen and protein source.

viii **Opportunity crop.** Where autumn sowing is impossible a spring cereal crop can be a profitable alternative.

ix The crop is in the ground for 6 months and allows another enterprise to use the land for the rest of the year.

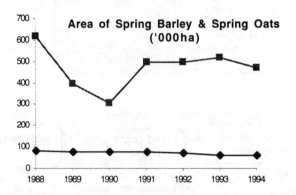

Area of Spring Barley & Spring Oats ('000ha)

KEY ASSESSMENT QUESTIONS

Yield is the key

i Is the site fertile, having a deep moisture retentive soil and a dry warm summer climate? If so, the following yields can be expected, in comparison with yields under average conditions.

Yields	Good t/ha	G.M. £/ha	Average t/ha	G.M. £/ha
Spring barley - malting	5.00	620	4.75	535
Spring oats - milling	5.75	590	4.70	590
Spring wheat - milling	6.25	680	5.25	530

Includes an area payment of £250/ha. (Adapted from J. Nix)

PRODUCTION

FACTORS AFFECTING CEREAL PROFITABILITY

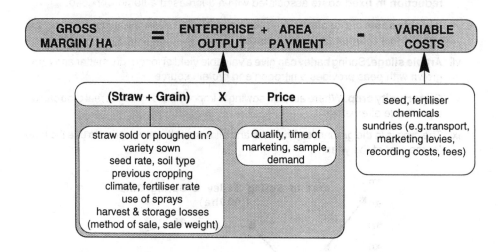

| GROSS MARGIN / HA | = | ENTERPRISE OUTPUT | + | AREA PAYMENT | − | VARIABLE COSTS |

(Straw + Grain) X **Price**

straw sold or ploughed in?
variety sown
seed rate, soil type
previous cropping
climate, fertiliser rate
use of sprays
harvest & storage losses
(method of sale, sale weight)

Quality, time of marketing, sample, demand

seed, fertiliser
chemicals
sundries (e.g.transport, marketing levies, recording costs, fees)

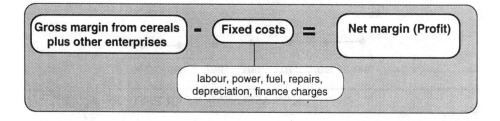

Gross margin from cereals plus other enterprises − **Fixed costs** = **Net margin (Profit)**

labour, power, fuel, repairs,
depreciation, finance charges

MARKETING

PRODUCTS

Primary Products

Grain This is either sold or used by the farmer.

Seed Strict quality controls apply when seed is sold - see page 7.

Feed Used in the production of animal feed on the farm or by compounders and sold back to farmers.

Secondary Products

Malting

Malting barley varieties (Winter & Spring) accounted for 52% of barley sowings in 1993/94. Spring varieties accounted for 61% of the malting area compared with 51% the previous year.

Milling

Spring wheat and oats are used for milling for human consumption (e.g. porridge and muesli, bread and biscuits). A few growers mill their own grain for specialised outlets, especially for stone ground or "organic" flour which commands a substantial premium.

MARKET OUTLETS

Usual Practice

Grain sold to local grain merchant either:
- i At the day's ("spot") price after harvest
- ii At an agreed ("forward") price before grain is harvested

Co-operatives

Members of grain co-ops use central storage to bulk up grain to achieve better prices. Co-ops can also offer central drying and cleaning facilities to improve grain quality and marketability.

Export And Intervention

Sales are usually done through merchants and other grain traders. They ensure grain meets minimum quality and quantity specifications. Production exceeds consumption in the UK by about 6m tonnes per annum and this surplus must either be exported or sold into intervention. Exports of wheat have recently broken previous records, and UK intervention cereal stocks are now at a low level totalling about 1.5m tonnes. (1.3mt barley and 170,000t wheat).

Futures

Futures are one means for growers to fix the sale price of their grain well in advance of harvest or even planting. These contracts are traded on the London Futures market through

MARKETING

brokers with traded options also being possible. Futures contracts provide the grower with price "insurance" . It is essential that professional Bank or Broker advice is sought before entering this market.

CONSUMPTION

Consumption of cereals for UK 1993/94:

	Human & industrial	Animal feed	Seed & other	Total m tonnes
Wheat	5.6	5.2	0.6	11.4
Barley	1.8	3.2	0.3	5.3
Oats	0.2	0.2	<0.1	0.4

Source N.F.U.

Prices £/tonne

Malting premiums can vary considerably from year to year according to quality and demand. By Mid December of 1992 good quality samples were fetching as much as £165/ tonne. In October of 1993, malting barley was trading at £112 - £118/tonne, compared to feed prices at £97 - £100/ tonne.

Intervention will be available from November to May 94/95. Monthly increments will be about £1.14 per month for feed barley starting at £102.04/tonne in November, rising to £108.85/ tonne the following May.

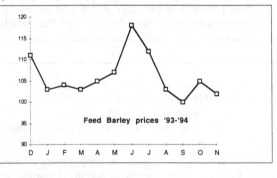

Feed Barley prices '93-'94

Spot prices before levies	Feed wheat	Feed barley	Milling wheat
Nov 1994 (£)	103	102	121

LEVIES AND QUOTAS

Co-responsibility - estimated to be about £10/t in 1992 but abolished from 1st July '92.

OUTSIDER'S GUIDE

1994 Season

Estimates of EU cereals production for the 1994 harvest indicate that the total production may be 162.8 million tonnes, lower than the 1993 harvest total of 164million tonnes by 1.3%.

SPRING CEREAL VARIETIES

Variety	Uses		
	Feeding	**Malting**	**Milling**
Barley	Hart Chad Tyne Nomad	(Triumph) (Blenheim) Alexis Prisma Chariot Dekado	
Wheat	varieties failing milling standards		Axona Canon Tonic Alexandia Baldus
Oats	Melys Valiant MInerva (Matra)		Rollo Dula Aberglen

Omission of certain varieties does not indicate their unsuitability.

MARKET REQUIREMENTS

All grain sold must meet the **required standard** (see page 8) for the market for which it is intended. Failure to do so incurs price penalties or even rejection.

Seed Corn

Usually produced to a Higher Voluntary Standard (HVS). Seed must be at least 98% **pure**, 85% **germination**, 15% **moisture**. No more than 0.5 **loose smut** or 10 seeds of any species per 500g is permitted. Seed crops must comply with certification standards enforced by official field inspectors.

Compounders

A maximum moisture content of 16% is usual. Grain to be sound and sweet, free from objectionable smell and taste. No heated grain or contamination (e.g. with ergot or insects).

MARKETING

MARKETS

Maltsters can be very demanding in their requirements which state: specific varieties, appearance - bright, well filled grain, moisture 16% maxmium, low nitrogen % ideally below 1.75, and 95% minimum germination. The distilling industry will only accept low nitrogen barleys, below 1.6% N. Changes in public taste from bitter to lager allows higher grain N samples to be used of between 1.6% and 1.75%. For Pale ale lower N content is required.

Millers specify variety, appearance and moisture, protein 11% minimum, Hagberg over 250 seconds and high specific weight.

When a farmer sells grain, it is sold on the basis that the sample is representative of the bulk of the grain which he is selling. The grain should be sound, of marketable quality and fit for the purpose for which it is sold and for storage.

COST OF MARKETING

Price received by farmer is often less than intervention or futures price because of the costs of:

> storage
> transport
> cleaning and drying charges
> commission
> co-responsibility levy *
> margins
> discount for low quality

* Co-responsibility Levy (discontinued after 1st July 1992).

This was a levy charged on EU producers of grain to discourage grain production. The amount of levy is related to the overall harvest amount in the previous year (1991 = 180.2 mt). It is charged on all sales from the farm; intervention, exports, and grain purchased by processors. Farmers selling less than 25 tonnes are exempt.

CONTRACTORS CHARGES (1993/94)

Grain Drying	£18.00/t to remove 5% moisture
Storage	30p/t per week
Cleaning on Farm	£15.50/t for seed
Transport 10 miles	£3.40/t
Transport 50 miles	£4.75/t

ENVIRONMENT

CLIMATE AND SOILS

Cereals generally do better in the drier eastern parts of the UK owing to easier harvest conditions and more flexible drilling season.

Wheat is favoured by heavier soils and **barley** does relatively better on light soils, both in terms of yield and quality:

e.g. **Spring wheat** may not reach the required protein content for breadmaking on light land. **Spring barley** rarely has a low enough nitrogen % on heavy land to reach malting standard.

Soil pH Sensitivity

Barley	is sensitive to acidity and can suffer below 6.5
Wheat	tolerates pH down to 6.0 without ill effect
Oats	are least sensitive, 5.5 is satisfactory

DRAINAGE AND IRRIGATION

Drainage

Optimum water table depth is **100-120 cm**. Spring cereals have low susceptibility to poor drainage. Germination and establishment are enhanced by the quicker warming of well drained soils.

Field Drainage Work

Drainage 1992: costs range from £1300 to £1500/acre for a full drainage scheme. Grants only available to replace existing systems, e.g 15% or 25% in LFA's.

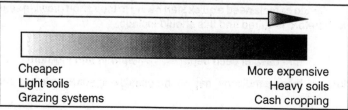

Cheaper	More expensive
Light soils	Heavy soils
Grazing systems	Cash cropping

ENVIRONMENT

ROTATIONS

Rotation - a three, four or five year cycle of different crops grown on a particular field is usually practised to maintain soil fertility, help weed control and prevent the build up of diseases which may favour certain crops. 15% of eligible crop, cereals and combinable break crops must now be set-aside.

Heavy Land

Year	
1	Winter wheat
2	Winter wheat or Spring wheat
3	Winter barley/set-aside
4	Oilseed rape

In this case the Spring wheat would allow serious grass weeds like black-grass to be tackled during a run of cereals (black-grass germinates in autumn, so is easily controlled during the winter prior to spring cereal sowing).

Light Land

Year	
1	Sugar beet
2	Spring barley/set-aside
3	Potatoes
4	Winter wheat
5	Winter barley

In this case, growing Spring barley would avoid the difficulty of establishing an Autumn sown crop following late harvested roots.

CULTIVATIONS

Spring cereals need a quick start owing to their short growing season. A good seedbed is therefore required and this should include:

fairly fine tilth	level surface
firm base at seed depth	warmth and moisture

Unfortunately these conditions may not be possible in some soils and seasons.

ENVIRONMENT

Drilling Date

An **early start** is beneficial and this is especially true of light land farms where the soil is workable earlier and where severe drought would be expected later.

Heavy land farmers find great difficulty in producing a seedbed until later in the year, and for this reason generally avoid spring cereals. Autumn ploughing of heavy land is essential to allow winter weather to produce a "frost mould" or tilth.

Most UK Spring wheat is Autumn/Winter drilled. The earlier establishment should encourage a longer growing season and higher yields while maintaining spring variety quality premiums. Harsh winters can lead to severe crop loss.

	SPRING BARLEY
Plant population:	250-300 plants/m²
Seedrate:	125-150 kg/ha (Higher for spring wheat 170-220kg/ha)
Drilling depth:	2.5 cm depth approximately
Row width:	10 -17 cm (narrow rows)
Post-establishment cultivation:	consolidate seedbed with cambridge roll - aids crop establishment, moisture retention and presses down stones

LEGAL ASPECTS

The farm environment and food production are increasingly controlled by statutory regulations e.g.

F.E.P.A: Food And Environment Protection Act (1985)

Chemical use restricted to approved crop/timing/dose rate. Conditions of chemical storage/handling/application/disposal subject to strict control.

Residues of chemicals in food subject to tight regulation and scrutiny.

Personnel require training and certification.

Water Quality Legislation

EU directives specify maximum residue levels e.g. nitrate: 50ppm. and any agrochemicals: 0.1ppm.

Leaving land bare over winter before establishing a Spring crop can lead to serious leaching problems, especially on light land. In future, farmers may be forced to grow cover-crops over winter to "mop-up" any available nitrogen.

ENVIRONMENT

Nitrate Sensitive Areas (NSA's)

A voluntary scheme was developed in the UK in 1990 for the investigation of nitrate losses. 10 nitrate sensitive areas were designated. Farmers who joined the scheme had to comply with a number of restrictions under the NVZ's. There are three options: the basic scheme (between £65 - £105/ha), converting intensive to extensive grassland (£250/ha), converting arable to extensive grassland with limited grazing (£340 - £440/ha).Nitrogen Sensitive Areas (N.S.A's)

PILOT NITRATE SCHEME 1989

Map marks Nitrate Sensitive Areas (Compensation Scheme)

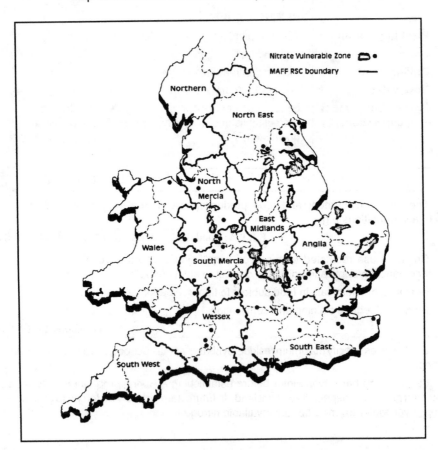

ENVIRONMENT

LEGAL ASPECTS

Sites Of Special Scientific Interest (S.S.S.I.'s)

These are areas of land and/or water that have Oeen declared as sites of outstanding wildlife or geological value by the Nature Conservancy Council. This may involve:

i   a survey carried out with the owner's permission.

ii three months notice of the proposal listing potentially damaging operations.

iii a management agreement which prevents some operations without prior consultation with the N.C.C.

iv reimbursement of any loss of income caused by a management agreement.

v   tax benefits and grants for conservation activities that enhance the value of the site.

 EQUIPMENT, COSTS AND WORK RATE

Equipment	Typical Cost (£)	Work Rate/day
Primary cultivations		
Sub-soiler (if soil compacted)	2,000	
4 furrow **plough (reversible)**	4,00 - 5,700	10 ha
100kW **tractor**	30,000 - 40,000	
Secondary cultivations		
Spring tined **cultivators**	3,000	20 ha
Power **harrow 3.5 - 4.0m**	3,500 - 6,000	10-15ha
Sowing		
Grain **drill**	2,300 - 6,000	10-15 ha
Combine drill	6,000	8-12 ha
Fertiliser **broadcaster**	1,500	20-30 ha
Full-width **spreaders**	5,000 - 6,500	20-30 ha
Contractors charges per hectare		
Ploughing	32.00 -40.00	
Cultivations (per operation)	25.00	
Combine drilling	26.00	
Spraying	9.90	

Source: adapted from A.B.C.

OUTSIDER'S GUIDE

ENVIRONMENT

1994 GROWING SEASON

After the difficult wet autumn in 1993, more spring crops were drilled than initially planned. Due to the wet soil conditions some crops were late drilled. Pests and disease levels were low and yields were slightly better then in 1993.

GROWTH STAGES

THE SPRING CEREAL PRODUCTION CYCLE

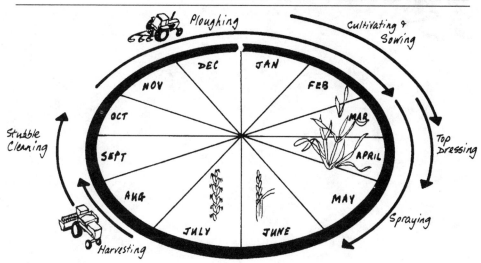

THE CEREAL GROWTH CYCLE

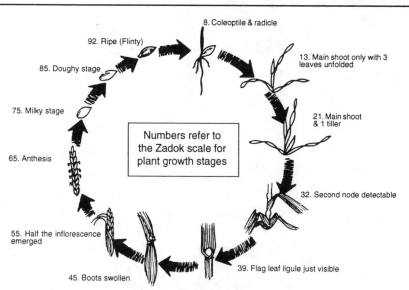

8. Coleoptile & radicle

92. Ripe (Flinty)

85. Doughy stage

75. Milky stage

65. Anthesis

55. Half the inflorescence emerged

45. Boots swollen

13. Main shoot only with 3 leaves unfolded

21. Main shoot & 1 tiller

32. Second node detectable

39. Flag leaf ligule just visible

Numbers refer to the Zadok scale for plant growth stages

OUTSIDER'S GUIDE

GROWTH STAGES

NUTRITION

Nitrogen

Cereals are very responsive to **nitrogen**, but too much can lead to **lodging** and **reduced yields.** The amount needed depends on previous cropping and soil type.

Phosphate And Potash

Large yield responses are unlikely unless soil levels are particularly low. **Normally maintenance dressings only** are required but it is essential to use **soil analysis** to determine the amount needed.

Requirements (Typical Amounts Applied)

Phosphate and Potash

Typical Yield Level (t/ha)	Phosphate (kg/ha)	Potash (kg/ha)
5.0	40	35

As yield increases, requirements for these nutrients will rise. Straw removal increases considerably the requirements for potash, particularly in barley and oats.

Nitrogen (kg/ha) for spring barley

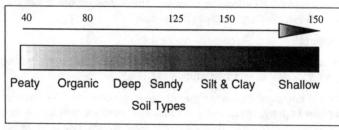

40	80	125	150	150

Peaty   Organic   Deep Sandy   Silt & Clay   Shallow
Soil Types

Spring wheat requirement is slightly higher (up to 170 kg/ha especially when autumn drilled) to enhance yield and grain protein level (bread making quality requirement).

Malting barley tends to be given lower rates hopefully to reduce N% content of grain. Lower N rates will reduce yield potential but with no guarantee of malting quality. Apply earlier in the season.

A break crop grown prior to the spring cereal will reduce the nitrogen requirement by about 40 kg/ha - 60kg/ha.

NUTRITION

TIMING APPLICATIONS

	Wheat	Barley & Oats
Nitrogen	Up to 70kg/ha at sowing depending on the date of sowing. Remainder at leaf sheath lengthening.	Generally any time from pre-sowing up to three leaf stage. If very early planted, at sowing up to 50 kg/ha. Rest at 3 leaf stage. For malting crops apply before mid - March to reduce risk of raising grain nitrogen %.
P & K	In **deficient** soils, nutrients should be applied at **sowing**. For soils higher in P & K, a maintenance dressing can be applied at any convenient time.	

MICRO NUTRIENTS

Magnesium

Deficiency symptoms - **yellowing between the veins of the leaves** - are rarely experienced. Seen most on sandy or acidic soils.

Trace elements

The most common reason for trace element deficiency is **over liming**, and this condition is especially associated with sandy, peat and calcinous soils.

The only two of any significance are **manganese** and **copper**. The immediate solution is a **leaf-applied spray**. Trace element **deficiencies** more noticable in spring cereals because of their **rapid growth**. If deficiency is seen, investigate through specialist **soil and crop analysis.**

	Crop	Deficiency symptoms
Manganese	Barley	light brown speckles
	Wheat	yellow mottling
	Oats	grey mottling
Copper	Cereals	white tip - leaf tip bleached and shivelled

NUTRITION

LEGAL ASPECTS

C.O.S.H.H. (Control Of Substances Hazardous To Health)

Regulations affect the storage and use of fertilizer to some extent:

Ammonium nitrate (fertilizer)

This is a fire hazard and hence an assessment of risk must be made under the regulations

Slurry

Any slurry storage presents potential hazards and a variety of provisions are necessary to minimise risks e.g. warning notices, child proof fencing

C.O.S.H.H.

These regulations place a duty on farmers to make an assessment of risk for each and every use of materials which could harm users or third parties. The procedure involves the following steps:

i   identify and list all likely pest problems

ii   assess alternatives to chemical application to check whether it is possible to avoid chemical use

iii identify alternative chemicals to do the job

iv   check the possible hazards in each case

v   assess the site of application (is it near habitation, footpath, livestock, inside a building, etc.)

vi   assess method of application

vii assess necessary precautions and safety equipment

viii choose the least hazardous alternative chemical method that will fulfil the required purpose

ix   choose appropriate safety equipment

x   re-check decision process.

(Source: British Agrochemicals Association Ltd. Plain Man's Guide to Pestcides and the C.O.S.H.H. Assessment.)

NUTRITION

WEED CONTROL

Economically, weeds are the most important crop protection problem in spring cereals. Control is usually necessary to prevent their **harmful effects** on:

> Yields
>
> Grain quality
>
> Ease of harvesting

Weed Competition

The severity of yield loss increases with weed numbers mainly due to competition for mineral nutrients (especially **nitrogen**) and for **moisture**.

Weed Types

Grass weeds, which are similar to cereals, tend to compete more effectively than broad leaf weeds.

Weeds	Yield response
Grass weeds	10-20%
Broad leaf weeds	2%

There are also differences in competition ability within these groups of weeds.

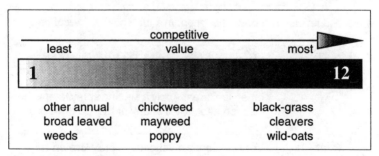

Weeds with high competitive value are potentially more damaging. For example, a **yield loss** of about 1 tonne/ha has been recorded for a high infestation of **black-grass**. In fact, black-grass is generally a much less common problem than in Winter cereals because:

    i   it is an Autumn germinator

    ii it is favoured by heavy soils

HEALTH

Spraying

This is not always cost effective in the short term but in the long term weed populations will rise if left uncontrolled.

Growing Spring cereals helps weed control
i Spring cereals are **more competitive** than Winter cereals due to their shorter seedling stage
ii Spring planting allows time for ploughing and **deep weed seed burial**
iii Spring cultivations discourage autumn germinating weeds
iv Weed control programmes are more effective because more **uniform weed germination**, and more spraying days when weeds are susceptible

DISEASE CONTROL

Most of the major spring cereal diseases are **fungal**. The main factors affecting the development of these diseases and their control using fungicides are outlined below. Barley Yellow Dwarf Virus is aphid transmitted and thus control of the aphid will prevent tramission of the disease, though timing is very difficult.

Economic Threshold

When disease levels are above the 'economic threshold' it is economic to treat. For example:

Disease	Economic threshold for Spring barley
Mildew	Spray as soon as it affects 1-3% of the lower green leaf area. Apply a second spray later if the disease affects 3% of any of the top three leaf area.
Rust	Very susceptible varieties - spray **Brown rust** as soon as disease is noticed. Spray other varieties only if disease is spreading.

Green Bridge Situation

When Spring barley is **grown next to Winter barley** diseases may spread from one crop to the other. **Mildew** especially, may carry over on Winter barley and act as source of early infection for the Spring crop.

HEALTH

Early Disease Development

Disease infections in early growth stages are most damaging and should be controlled.

High Nitrogen Application

High nitrogen rates encourages a **lush dense crop** - an ideal micro-climate for disease development. Nitrogen reduces cell wall thickness and increases disease susceptibility.

Appropriate Weather

Certain weather favours specific diseases:

Disease	Weather conditions	Crops affected
Mildew	warm & humid	wheat & barley
Y.Rust	cool & moist	wheat & barley
B.Rust	warm & moist	wheat & barley
Crown Rust	warm & wet	oats
S.tritici	cool & wet May-June	wheat
Rhynchosp.	cool & wet	barley

PEST CONTROL

Previous history of pest damage is important. Preventative measures can be taken when pest problems are predictable. It is often more economic to assess the risk of attack than to make routine treatments.

Economic Thresholds

These are available and indicate the levels of infestation above which the use of pesticides will be cost effective. A.D.A.S. provide warnings of likely infestations within any U.K. area.

HEALTH

Damage, Occurrence And Identification

Damage	Pest	Crop	Occurrence
Seed hollowed out	slugs	S Wheat	especially on heavy soil crops after break
	wireworms	all	following grass
Shoot damage below soil surface	slugs	all	(see above)
	leatherjacket	all	following grass
	wireworms	all	following grass
	frit-fly	oats	following grass
Seedling damage	slugs	all	(see above)
	leatherjacket	all	following grass
	wireworms	all	following grass
'Dead-hearts'	wheat bulb fly	wheat	following fallow or early harvested crop
	frit-fly	all	following grass
Damage to ear	aphids	all	erratic
	frit-fly	oats	following grass
	thrips	all	erratic

EQUIPMENT, COSTS AND WORK RATE

Equipment	Typical cost	Work rate /hour
Crop sprayer		
600 - 800 litres	£2,500 - 10,000	4 ha
1500 - 2000 litres	£6,500 - 21,500	8 ha
Contractors' rates spraying operation	**Cost £/ha**	
Standard (225l/ha)	9.88 (£16/hr)	
Low ground pressure	11.00 (£17.80/hr)	

LEGAL ASPECTS

Crop protection has become the object of much recent legislation. Two sets of regulations in particular restrict the freedom of farmers and chemical companies in this area:

F.E.P.A: Food And Environment Protection Act (1985)

F.E.P.A. regulations make the following main demands:

i   that operators of equipment for applying specified chemicals must pass a 2 stage test of knowledge and proficiency before becoming qualified to use the equipment unsupervised

ii that only M.A.F.F. approved chemicals may be used and only at approved rates and times to specified crops

iii that chemicals be stored, handled, applied and disposed of in an approved safe manner

iv that food products be tested and meet strict standards of residue contamination.

C.O.S.H.H.

These regulations place a duty on farmers to make an assessment of risk for each and every use of materials which could harm users or third parties. (See page 19 for further details.)

Sites Of Special Scientific Interest (S.S.S.I.'s)

These are areas of land and/or water that have been declared as sites of outstanding wildlife or geological value by the Nature Conservancy Council. This may involve:

i   a survey carried out with the owner's permission

ii three months notice of the proposal lifting potentially damaging operations

iii a management agreement which prevents some operations without prior consultation with the N.C.C.

iv reimbursement of any loss of income caused by a management agreement

v   tax benefits and grants for conservation activities that enhance the value of the site.

HEALTH

HARVESTING

AIM

Harvest cereals when the grains have completely **filled** and **dried** so that the water content is **below 16%**. This moisture % permits safe storage following harvest.

After grain maturity, harvesting requires a **dry period of a day or two** (depending upon wind strength) to dry any water from rain or dew still present on plants which will pass through the harvester.

TIMING CRITERIA

Too early	Too late
High number of green grains	shedding losses likely
Drying & storage problems	poorer quality samples
Low specific weight	more likely discoloured
Difficult to thresh	sprouting grains

Despite the problems of early harvesting, the crop might still be taken early...

Reasons For Harvesting Early

i   limited drying capacity

ii allow timely entry of following crop

iii avoid shedding

Visual Assessment

Crop	Straw	Ears
Wheat	mainly light yellow	golden with a proportion able to be snapped off in good conditions
Barley	mainly light yellow	bent over so that very few show across field
Oats	still slightly green	golden with top grains ripe and bottom grains slightly immature left longer and top grains will shed

HARVESTING

Hand Assessment

Grain can be rubbed out easily from the chaff

Grain too hard to be dented with thumb nail, but not "flinty" (shiny) when cracked open

Moisture Content

Dry years: leave until 16% moisture providing there is no shedding of grains

Wet years: harvest when ripe if crop can be dried

QUALITY CRITERIA

Variety

First harvest those with least resistance to ear loss or shedding of grains.

Market

Feed: low priority - lowest quality grain

Milling: in wet years harvest early as this gives a higher Hagberg number for better quality bread

Malting: preserve germination ability by timely harvest

Seed: harvest before any sprouting risk

Other factors

Combine settings - ensure properly set and sieves clean to minimise grain losses and damage.

Weather effects - wet grain is difficult to thresh and dry grain is more easily cracked or damaged.

POST HARVEST

Stubble Hygiene

This is the removal of weeds and 'volunteer' cereals (reducing the risk of disease carry over).

Methods:

i   **cultivations**: ploughing and/or shallow cultivation. Conditions must be dry repeated cultivations necessary

ii   **herbicides**: saves time, labour, fuel, machinery costs

contact herbicides: economic to use on annual weeds. These work on contact with the plant, and good plant coverage is needed to be effective.

systemic herbicides: more effective and usually essential for perennial weeds. The chemical is absorbed into the plant, and moves within it to disrupt plant growth.

Many herbicides now combine systemic and contact action.

Residue Disposal

By incorporation and baling

Effect on	Type of effect	
	Incorporate	Bale
Reducing pest/disease	Bad	None
Reducing slugs	Bad	None
Drainage/soil structure	V.Good	Bad
Minimum cultivations	Bad	None
Following crop	Bad	None
Nutrient return	Good	Bad

In **1992, burning was banned** due to recent legislation (1989).

STORAGE

For safe storage grain should be kept cool and dry. Generally grain will store safely up to 15°C and 15% moisture.

Other storage options include sealed storage of moist grain or treatment with propionic acid (e.g. "Propcorn") to prevent deterioration. However, grain stored by these methods is suitable only for animal feed.

Pre-Cleaning

Passing grain through a machine to remove trash, green material, weed seeds, etc. reduces the moisture content and reduces the drying requirements.

HARVESTING

Drying

Two systems are used: Hot air driers and Ambient air driers. The more common system uses blown or sucked air at ambient temperature, into bins as shown in the diagram.

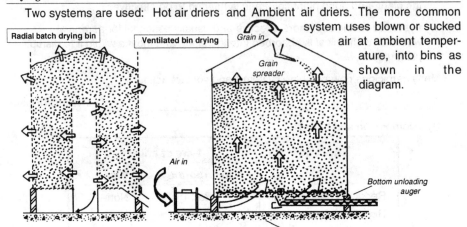

Radial batch drying bin

Ventilated bin drying

Grain in

Grain spreader

Air in

Bottom unloading auger

Counter flow drying unit

Alternatively, grain may be stored on the floor over air ducts or mesh flooring through which ambient air is pumped.

ON-FLOOR DRIERS

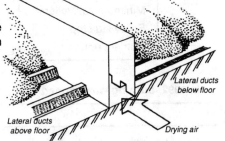

Lateral ducts below floor

Lateral ducts above floor

Drying air

Sources Of Damage During Storage:

Source of loss	Condition
Mould	damp grain (above 15% moisture).
Insects	warm (above 15ºC).
Mites	most conditions except very dry and cold.

Safe Storage Life (Wheat)

Moisture content %	Grain temperature	
	10ºC	20ºC
17.5	11 weeks	3.5 weeks
15.5	38 weeks	13 weeks

HARVESTING

Store Hygiene

The aim is to exclude insect pests and mites. This requires:

i sound **structure** - no cracks etc. to harbour insects

ii **brush** and vacuum before use

iii **spray appropriate chemical** before use

iv mix **insecticide** with grain if pest problems are likely

v ensure grain is **clean**, **dry** and **cool** before entry

Monitoring And Sampling

Grain can deteriorate quickly so monitor regularly, with many sample points, at varying depths using a 'grain spear'.

i plot grain temperature and moisture over time -beware a sudden rise

ii examine samples for pest activity and mould

EQUIPMENT, COSTS AND WORK RATE

Equipment	Typical Cost (£)	Work Rate/hr
Combine harvester 3.6-4.9m	50-70000	1.5 ha
Grain trailers	5000	-
Straw baler (big/high capacity)	9000-15000	1.0 ha
Bale handling equipment	2500	-
Straw chopper	3500	-
Grain drier (mobile)	30000	10 tonnes
Grain store on floor= £50-220/tonne	store capacity	-
Grain movement equipment	4500	40 tonnes

Contractors charges	£
Combining	82.00/ha
Pick up baling	0.18/bale
Combining & carting	106.25.00/ha
Straw chopping	29.05/ha

HARVESTING

LEGAL ASPECTS

Storage Pest Control

Restrictions will now be placed on insecticide treatment of stored grain owing to the strict regulations on pesticide residues. Increasingly, emphasis will be on prevention.

Grain Passport

A grain 'passport' must now accompany any grain sold. This states details of any chemical storage treatment used.

OUTSIDER'S GUIDE

KEY ASSESSMENT QUESTIONS

Factors Affecting Yield

Soil type

Heavy land	is often unsuited to spring sowing and can give rise to poor results due to cloddy seed-bed and late sowing. However, when the crop is sown satisfactorily, clay soils yield good wheat crops.
Light sandy soil	generally gives rather poor yields due to moisture stress and possibly to nutrient deficiency. Barley does better than wheat.
Medium (loam) soils	are generally better yielding than either extreme. Grow wheat or barley.
Chalky soils	suit barley particularly well and typically grow good malting samples and high yields.
Silts	are ideal for spring wheat but seldom used due to more profitable cropping possibilities.

Input level

Spring cereals are regarded as low input crops and do not respond economically to high cost production systems.

Drilling date

Very important influence on yield. Early drilling gives:

> longer growing season
>
> establishment of good roots before dry season
>
> but may encourage more fungal disease.

Variety

Roughly 10% difference between highest and lowest yielders on NIAB list.

Disease and weed levels

These vary with site, previous cropping, varietal choice and success of control measures.

PERFORMANCE

SEASON

Perhaps the most important determinant of yield. The best conditions include:

> dry early spring
>
> early warm up
>
> frequent showers between dry spells
>
> cool July during grainfill
>
> warm dry August for harvest

FACTORS AFFECTING PRICE

Season

Market price reflects intervention price, but can exceed it in years of good export trade and moderate production level (like 1990).

 Intervention Price For Feed Wheat And Barley 1994/5 (£)

Intervention price for all cereals	
November 1994 (£)	102.04
May 1995 (£)	108.85

 #### Quality

Milling wheat normally commands a premium over feed. In the 1994/95 season this is by £15 (Oct/Nov) per tonne.

Milling oats normally commands a premium over feed of £2 - £8 per tonne.

Malting barley of the best quality is always in strong demand and receives a premium of up to £20 - £35 per tonne over feed quality. Normally sold early in the season. However, due to variety and reduced nitrogen level applied, there is typically a yield penalty from growing malting barley.

Time of sale

Price normally rises after harvest by an amount roughly equating to the cost of storage. Intervention price rises by monthly increments of about £1.13t/month.

Co-responsibility levy

Levy varies annually according to stabiliser arrangements (see ⌂). Basic level for 1992/93 was estimated to be £10/t for the UK CRL stopped 1st July 1992.

GROSS MARGINS

Typical Average Gross Margins

		Barley	Wheat	Oats
Yield (Tonnes/ha)	Feed	5.00	5.25	4.75
	Malting	4.15		
Price £/t	Feed	87	90	92.5
	Milling		104	100
	Malting	104		
Output £	Feed	685	723	690
	Milling		796	725
	Malting	685		
Variable costs £	Seed	50	57.5	57.5
	Fert	52	65.0	40.0
	Sprays	48	72.5	37.5
Total V. Cost £ (straw retained)		150	195	135

* These figures include Area Payment of £250/ha.

Gross Margin £/ha

	Feed	535	528	555
	Milling		601	590
	Malting	535		

Adapted from : J. Nix 1994

FIXED COSTS

Profitable farms manage to **minimise fixed costs**, and to **maximise output** from their type of farming system so that fixed costs per unit output are as low as possible.

The figures below are typical levels of fixed costs for a specialist cereal farm. Individual farms will vary in their levels of fixed costs for specific reasons - e.g. new farms will have high **rental charges of 40% to 70%** higher than those quoted. **Larger farms** will tend to have lower fixed costs/hectare.

PERFORMANCE

Mainly Cereal Farm of 120 - 240 ha

(> 70% land for combinable crops)

Fixed costs:	£ / Hectare
Regular labour	150
Depreciation	95
Repairs, tax and insurance - equipment	50
Fuel and electricity	32
Contract charges - hedging/ditching	12
Land maintenance (fencing, repairs etc).	15
Rent & rates	115
Fees, office expenses	40
TOTAL	**509**

Adapted from: A.B.C.

Average Tenant's Capital

This is the value of investment normally provided by the tenant such as machinery, crops in store and other assets required to run the business.

Mainly Cereals Farm	£/ha
Livestock	225
Crops and cultivations	390
Machinery & equipment	575
TOTAL	**1190**

Adapted from: A.B.C.

THE
OUTSIDER'S GUIDE
to
WINTER CEREALS

1995 Edition

PRODUCTION

WORLD

Far more winter cereals are grown than spring sown cereals throughout the world owing to their higher yield potential under good growing conditions. However, they do tend to be more expensive to grow and rely on their great yield potential for success.

Total Cereal Production

CROP	PRODUCTION Million tonnes
Wheat	560
Coarse grains	786

Source: USDA.

EU

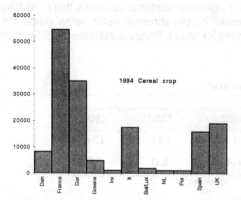

Million tonnes produced

Source Inside Track

1994 Cereal crop

Total cereal production in Europe is estimated to be 162 million tonnes (1994). The proportion provided by these major growers is shown in the pie chart.

1994 production in the EU is expected to be down by 2mt. In the UK, the cereal area was down by 11.6% due to the introduction of set-aside. The UK wheat acreage was down 14.8% at 1.76m ha and barley was down 10.3% at 1.16m ha.

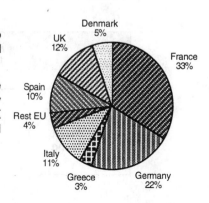

OUTSIDER'S GUIDE

PRODUCTION

UK

Production varies between about 19.5 million (1993) and 26.6 million tonnes (1984) according to the seasonal yield variation and the area under cereals. UK is now a net exporter of grain. The 1994 harvest estimate is 19.9 million tonnes, 2.5% increase on 1993. The trade balance of 5.8 million tonnes will be sold into intervention or exported.

U.K. wheat & barley exports

Yield

The record year is still 1984. However, ignoring seasonal variations there has been a steady increase over the longer term of about 2% per annum in winter cereal yields. MAFF estimates the likely size to be 13.4m tonnes for wheat. Barley is estimated at 5.9m tonnes and oats at 700,000t in '94.

UK Cereals Production Statistics ('000 tonnes)

Crop	1992	1993	1994
Wheat	14.1	12.9	13.4
Barley	7.4	6.0	5.9

Source: HGCA

	June 1993 million ha	June 1994 million ha
Total Cereals	3.03	3.05
Wheat	1.76	1.82
Barley total	1.16	1.10
Winter	0.64	0.62
Spring	0.52	0.47
Oats	0.09	0.11

Source: MAFF June Census

WHY GROW WINTER CEREALS ?

i   relatively good gross margin compared with alternative spring sown combinable crops

ii low fixed costs compared with roots and other intensive cash crops

iii can be grown in close succession without the pest and disease problems associated with monocropping non-cereal crops, with the exception of take-all disease

iv climatically much better suited than grassland to large areas of the drier eastern counties

v   relatively reliable yield, subject to less annual variability than many other crops

vi have wide soil tolerance

vii there is simply no viable alternative use for much of the eastern counties

FACTORS AFFECTING PROFITABILITY

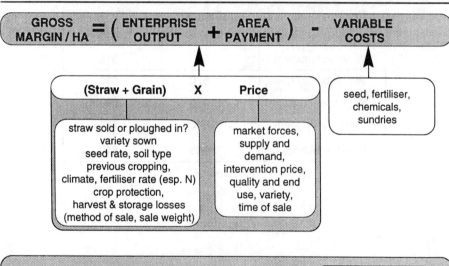

$$\text{GROSS MARGIN / HA} = \left(\text{ENTERPRISE OUTPUT} + \text{AREA PAYMENT} \right) - \text{VARIABLE COSTS}$$

(Straw + Grain)   X   Price

straw sold or ploughed in?
variety sown
seed rate, soil type
previous cropping,
climate, fertiliser rate (esp. N)
crop protection,
harvest & storage losses
(method of sale, sale weight)

market forces,
supply and
demand,
intervention price,
quality and end
use, variety,
time of sale

seed, fertiliser,
chemicals,
sundries

Gross margin from cereals plus other enterprises − Fixed costs = Net margin (Profit)

labour, power, fuel, repairs,
depreciation, finance charges

PRODUCTION

KEY ASSESSMENT QUESTIONS

i   **Soil type and yield** - for example: wheat yields

SOIL TYPE	Feature	Average Yield t/ha	Target Yield
Good fen silts	Retains moisture	9	10+
Clays and clay loams	Less water	7.5	9.5
Sandy loams Shallow light soils	retained	6.0	7.0
Sands		5.0	6.0

ii   **Gross margins (£/ha):-**

Crop	Average	Good
Winter wheat (feed)	680	815
W. wheat (milling)	680	815
Winter barley (feed)	570	680
W. barley (malting)	570	680
Winter oats (feed)	640	755
W. oats (Milling)	685	810

Source: Nix '94

MARKETING

PRODUCTS

Primary Products

Grain This is either sold or used by the farmer as seed for future crops or included in livestock rations.

Seed Strict quality controls apply before grain certified for seed which is required for it to be sold as seed.

Feed Used in the production of animal feed on the farm or by compounders and sold back to farmers.

Secondary Products

Malting . Currently 20% of the UK crop is used by maltsters. There is a strong export demand (20% of total malting barley production). Quality includes appearance, moisture %, Nitrogen content (ideally 1.5 - 1.6% N), and germination % is an important factor.

Milling. Wheat and Oats are used for milling for human consumption (e.g. bread and biscuits), porridge and muesli. A few growers mill their own grain for specialised outlets, especially for stone ground or "organic" flour which may command a substantial premium.

MARKET OUTLETS

Usual Practice

Grain sold to local grain merchant either:
- i at the day's ("spot") price after harvest
- ii at an agreed ("forward") price before or after grain is harvested.

Co-operatives

Members of grain co-ops use central storage to bulk up grain to achieve better prices. Co-ops can also offer central drying and cleaning facilities to improve grain quality and marketability.

Export And Intervention

Sales are usually done through merchants and other grain traders. They ensure grain meets minimum quality and quantity specifications. Production exceeds consumption in the UK by up to 6m tonnes per annum and this surplus must either be exported or sold into intervention.

Since July 1993 intervention stocks have been reduced from 33 million tonnes to 13 million tonnes due mainly to set-aside. The 3% reduction in set-aside in 1995 should result in a slight net increase.

MARKETING

Futures (Contracts)

Futures are one means for growers to fix the sale price of their grain well in advance of harvest or even planting. These contracts are traded on the London futures market through brokers with traded options also being possible. Futures contracts provide the grower with price "insurance". It is essential that professional Bank or Broker advice is sought before entering this market.

CONSUMPTION & USES OF CEREALS 1994/95

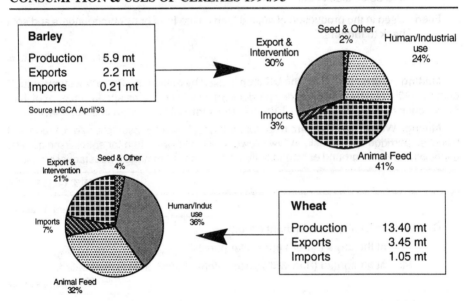

Barley

Production	5.9 mt
Exports	2.2 mt
Imports	0.21 mt

Source HGCA April'93

Wheat

Production	13.40 mt
Exports	3.45 mt
Imports	1.05 mt

Prices (£/tonne)

The co-responsibility levy was abolished as from 1st July 1992.

Intervention will be available from November to May 94/95. Monthly increments in intervention price will be about £1.14 per month.

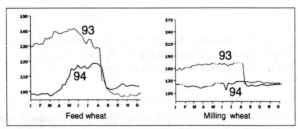

Buying in prices for breadmaking wheat and feed barley will start at £102.04/tonne in Nov 1993 rising to £108.85 per tonne delivered to store in May 1994.

MARKETING

Spot prices before levies	Feed wheat	Feed barley	Milling wheat
Oct 1994 (£)	103.2	101.5	120.8

PENALTIES

The UK has been divided in 7 yield regions for the Arable Aid Payment Scheme (AAPS). Base areas have been allocated to each region based on the average planting of cereals, oilseeds and pulse crops plus set-aside over the years 1989 to 1991. This base area is the maximum area on which Arable Aid Payments can be made. If there is an overshoot of the base area aid will be reduced and there could be additional uncompensated set-aside in the following year.

CEREAL VARIETIES

Variety	Uses			
	Feeding	Both	Malting	Milling
Barley	Pastoral Fighter Intro Target Gaelic Epic Manitou Willow	Puffin	Puffin Pipkin Halycon	
Wheat	Beaver Haven Riband Brigadier Hunter Buster Hussar			Mercia Genesis Hereward Spark Cadenza
Oats (* naked oats)	Mirabel Pendragon* Kynon* Aintree Gerald			Solva Image Craig Chamois

* husk falls off during the harvest

MARKETING

Winter wheat variety market share '94

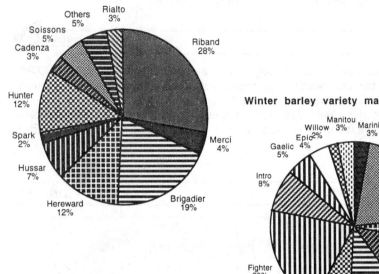

Winter barley variety market share '94

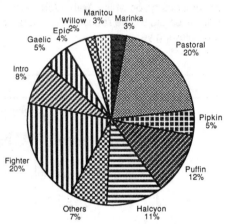

MARKET REQUIREMENTS

All grain sold must meet the **required standard** for the market for which it is intended. Failure to do so incurs price penalties or even rejection.

Seed Corn

Usually produced to a Higher Voluntary Standard (HVS). Seed must be at least 98% pure, 85% germination, 15% moisture. No more than 0.5 loose smut or contain more than 6 seeds of other cultivated cereal species, or 2 seeds of brome or couch species or 2 of any other weed species in a 2kg sample to meet certified seed 2nd generation standards at the Higher Voluntary standard.

Compounders

A maximum moisture content of 16% is usual. Grain to be sound and sweet, free from objectionable smell and taste. No heated grain or contamination (e.g. with ergot or insects).

MARKETING

MARKETS

Maltsters can be very demanding in their requirements which state: specific variety; appearance - bright, well-filled grain, moisture 16% maximum, low Nitrogen % (normally below 1.75%); and 95% minimum germination.

Millers specify variety, appearance and moisture, protein quantity (11% minimum, at 14%mc) and quality, Hagberg falling number over 250 seconds (indicates how well dough will rise), specific weight (76kg/hl).

When a farmer sells grain, it is sold on the basis that the sample is representative of the bulk of the grain which he is selling. The grain should be sound, of marketable quality and fit for the purpose for which it is sold and for storage.

COST OF MARKETING

The price received by the farmer is often less than intervention or futures price because of the costs of:

> **storage**
> **transport**
> **cleaning and drying charges**
> **commission**
> **margins**
> **discount for low quality**

CONTRACTORS CHARGES (1994)

Grain Drying by 3%	£7.00 - £7.75/t
Grain Drying by 7%	£7.75 - £8.50/t
Storage	20 - 30p/t per week
Cleaning on Farm	£15.50/t for seed
Transport 10 miles	£3.30/t - £3.40/t
Transport 50 miles	£4.50 - £4.90/t

Source: ABC No 38

MARKETING

ENVIRONMENT

CLIMATE AND SOILS

Cereals generally do better in the drier parts of the UK (shown in the map below) owing to easier harvest conditions and more flexible drilling season.

Wheat is favoured by heavier soils and **barley** does relatively better on light soils, both in terms of yield and quality:

e.g. **Wheat** may not reach the required protein content for bread-making on light land. **Barley** rarely has a low enough Nitrogen % on heavy land to reach malting standard.

Soil pH Sensitivity

Barley	is sensitive to acidity and can suffer below 6.5 (i.e. acid soil)
Wheat	tolerates pH down to 6.0 without ill effect.
Oats	are least sensitive to acid soils and pH 5.5 is satisfactory

DRAINAGE AND IRRIGATION

Drainage

Winter cereals suffer badly from waterlogging. Roots stunted by oxygen starvation during the winter fail to supply the crop with water in dry weather. Crops in badly waterlogged ground can lose almost 100% of their yield.

Field Drainage Work

Drainage 1992: £1300 - £1500/ha for a full drainage scheme

Cheaper	More expensive
Light soils	Heavy soils
Grazing systems	Cash cropping

Grants only available to replace drainage. e.g. 25% in LFA's and 15% elsewhere.

OUTSIDER'S GUIDE

ENVIRONMENT

ROTATIONS

Rotation - a three, four or five year cycle of different crops grown on a particular field is usually practised to maintain soil fertility, help weed control and prevent the build up of diseases which may favour certain crops.

Winter cereal growing is the basis of most arable systems.

Winter Wheat fits into many different types of cropping sequences, including:-

1	Continuous wheat	
2	Wheat - wheat - set-aside - beans	**Heavy land**
3	Wheat - potatoes - wheat - vegetables	**Silt**
4	Wheat - wheat - sugar beet - set-aside - peas	**Medium / light soil**

Winter Barley

Normally grown on the lighter land, though it has a special function in heavy land rotations as the preferred crop before oilseed rape (due to its early harvest), e.g.

1	W. wheat - w.barley - peas - w.barley - potatoes	**Light soil**
2	W. wheat - w. barley -set-aside - OSR	**Heavy land**

N.B.: Growers are now turning to early varieties of Wheat as an entry for OSR because of the greater gross margin potential.

CULTIVATIONS

Winter cereals are established by three different systems:-

> i   **conventional: Ploughing & secondary cultivation**
>
> ii   **minimal cultivations: Surface cultivation without ploughing. Possibly also after thorough straw incorporation**
>
> iii   **direct drilling: Seed drilled straight into stubble of previous crop with no prior cultivation**

ENVIRONMENT

Conventional System

More costly and time consuming but allows complete burial of surface trash and straw. Gives good control of difficult grass weeds (e.g. black-grass, sterile brome) relieves compaction and gives a level surface when well done.

Minimal Cultivations

The preferred system on heavy land, because it avoids ploughing up clods that are difficult to break down. Saves time, fuel and machinery wear, but may encourage weeds and diseases.

Direct Drilling

Fast and cost effective, providing soil is not prone to compaction, and is level and free from trash and established weeds. A popular technique in the 1970's may be considered in the 1990's to reduce fixed costs.

Sowing

Seed should be sown to the following standards:

Depth	2.5 - 3.5 cm
Width between rows	10 - 17 cm
Plant population (established plants)	250 - 350/m²
Seed rate	160 - 250 kg/ha

Optimal Drilling Dates

Winter barley	20 September to 5 October
Winter wheat	25 September to 15 October

Much wheat is drilled after the optimum period when it follows root crops. The latest recommended date for drilling most varieties of winter cereals following root crops is the end of January. There is no cut off date for Cadenza.

ENVIRONMENT

Environment 1993/4 Season

Despite the wet autumn and subsequent late drilling followed by an early summer drought average yields were harvested (except on the light sands). Incidence of more pests (except slugs) and disease were below average.

Grain quality was good. Use of home grown wheat for milling will be higher this season (83% in 1994/5 compared with 72% in 1993/94) but milling premiums are lower on average (£15/tonne). Malting premiums are high, up to £35/t.

 ## LEGAL ASPECTS

The farm environment and food production are increasingly controlled by statutory regulations .

FEPA: Food And Environment Protection Act (1985)

Chemical use restricted to approved crop/timing/dose rate. Conditions of chemical storage/handling/application/disposal subject to strict control.

Residues of chemicals in food subject to tight regulation and scrutiny.

Personnel require training and certification.

Scheme is found to be effective.

Water Quality Legislation

In 1991 the nitrate directive was agreed by the EU. Member states are required to designate nitrate vulnerable zones (NVZ's) where the nitrate concentration in water exceeded 50mg/l.

MAFF and the NRA have designated 72 NVZ's in England and Wales and 2 in Scotland. These designated areas are under review. Farmers in NVZ's will have to comply with a number of restrictions based on the The Code of Good Agricultural Practice for the protection of water.

Restrictions include: Inorganic fertilizer - amount and timing, application of organic manure and storage of slurry and silage. No compensation available.

Nitrate Sensitive Areas (NSA's)

A voluntary scheme was developed in the UK in 1990 for the investigation of nitrate losses. 10 nitrate sensitive areas were designated. Farmers who joined the scheme had to comply with a number of restrictions under the NVZ's. There are three options: the basic scheme (between £65 - £105/ha), converting intensive to extensive grassland (£250/ha), converting arable to extensive grassland with limited grazing (£340 - £440/ha).

ENVIRONMENT

PILOT NITRATE SCHEME

Map marks Nitrate Sensitive Areas (compensation Scheme)

EQUIPMENT, COSTS AND WORK RATE

Equipment	Typical cost £'000	Work rate ha/day
Primary cultivations		
sub-soiler (if soil compacted)	1.7 - 2.2	10 -15
4 furrow Plough	4.5 - 15.0	10
100kW tractor (4WD)	33.0 - 40.0	
Secondary cultivations		
Spring-tined cultivators	3.4 - 3.6	20
Power harrow (3.5 - 4 m)	5.0 - 6.0	10 - 15
Sowing		
Grain drill (4 m)	6.0	10 - 15
Combined grain & fertilizer	7.5	8 - 12
Fertiliser broadcaster	1.5	20 - 30
Full-width spreaders	5.0 - 6.5	20 - 30
Sprayer mounted 800 l	2.5 - 3.0	30 - 40

Contractors charges £ / hectare	
Ploughing	30.20
Cultivations*	25.00
Combine drilling	26.00
Spraying	9.90
*per operation	

Note: Costs vary greatly due to size, specification, discounts (33%!).
Work rates vary according to operator skills, field sizes, soil type, power unit, length of working day.

ENVIRONMENT

Sites Of Special Scientific Interest (SSSI's)

These are areas of land and/or water that have been declared as sites of outstanding wildlife or geological value by the Nature Conservancy Council. This may involve:

i   a survey carried out with the owner's permission

ii   three months notice of the proposal listing potentially damaging operations

iii   a management agreement which prevents some operations without prior consultation with the N.C.C.

iv   reimbursement of any loss of income caused by a management agreement

v   tax benefits and grants for conservation activities that enhance the value of the site

THE WINTER CEREAL PRODUCTION CYCLE

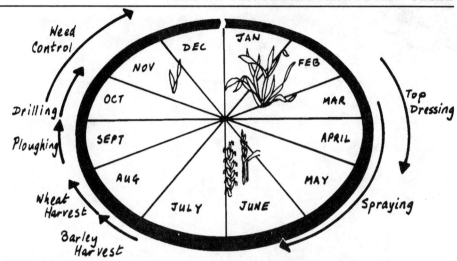

THE WINTER CEREAL GROWTH CYCLE

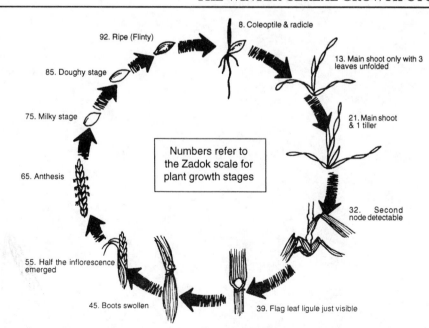

8. Coleoptile & radicle

13. Main shoot only with 3 leaves unfolded

21. Main shoot & 1 tiller

32. Second node detectable

39. Flag leaf ligule just visible

45. Boots swollen

55. Half the inflorescence emerged

65. Anthesis

75. Milky stage

85. Doughy stage

92. Ripe (Flinty)

Numbers refer to the Zadok scale for plant growth stages

OUTSIDER'S GUIDE

GROWTH STAGES

NUTRITION

GENERAL

Nitrogen

Cereals are very responsive to **nitrogen**, but too much can lead to **lodging** and **reduced yields.** The amount of nitrogen needed depends on previous cropping, soil type and expected yield.

Phosphate And Potash

Large yield responses are unlikely unless soil levels are particularly low. **Normally maintenance dressings only** are required but it is essential to use **soil analysis** to determine the amount needed.

Requirements (Typical Amounts Applied)

Phosphate and Potash

Kg/ha (winter wheat cereals assuming straw removed and yields of 7.5 t/ha)

Index	0	1	2	3	over 3
P : K	120 : 140	95 : 115	70: 90	70 : 0	0 : 0

As yield increases, requirements for these nutrients will also rise. Straw removal increases considerably the requirements for potash. More potash is removed in barley straw than in wheat straw.

Nitrogen

There are wide variations in nitrogen requirement between different situations. Wheat generally needs higher rates than barley or oats because it has stronger straw and yields more heavily. The use of organic manures will reduce the nutrient requirements

Previous crop	N Index	W. Wheat	W. Barley Feed	W. Barley Malting
Cereals	0	175 - 225	160 - 200	110 - 120
Break crops	1	90 - 190	120 - 160	60 - 80
Grass	2	0 - 130	40 - 100	40

NUTRITION

Sulphur

With the reductions in atmospheric sulphur, sulphur may be required in the future especially on sandy or shallow soils over chalk.

Micro Nutrients

Magnesium

Deficiency symptoms - yellowing between the veins of the leaves - are rarely experienced. Seen most on sandy or acidic soils.

Trace Elements

The most common reason for trace element deficiency is over-liming, and this condition is typically associated with sandy and peaty soils.

The only two of any significance are **manganese** and **copper**. The immediate solution is a leaf-applied spray. Trace element deficiencies in winter cereals are less noticeable than in spring cereals because of their slower growth. If deficiency is seen, investigate through specialist soil and crop analysis.

Element	Crop	Deficiency symptoms
Manganese	Barley	light brown speckles
	Wheat	yellow mottling
	Oats	grey mottling
Copper	Cereals	white tip - leaf tip bleached and shrivelled

 Growth Regulators

Applied at the end of tillering or later in the season to barleys (especially 6 - rows) to shorten and stiffen straw to prevent lodging and ear loss.

Weak strawed wheat varieties and early drilled crops would likewise benefit. Often used to keep milling wheat varieties standing and thus maintain their quality.

Growth regulators include Cycocel, Terpal, Cerone, Upgrade.

NUTRITION

LEGAL ASPECTS

C.O.S.H.H. (Control Of Substances Hazardous To Health)

Regulations affect the storage and use of fertilizer to some extent:

Ammonium nitrate (fertilizer)

This is a fire hazard and hence an assessment of risk must be made under the regulations.

Slurry

Any slurry storage presents potential hazards and a variety of provisions are necessary to minimise risks e.g. warning notices, child proof fencing.

C.O.S.H.H.

These regulations place a duty on farmers to make an assessment of risk for each and every use of materials which could harm users or third parties. The procedure involves the following steps:

i   identify and list all likely pest problems

ii   assess alternatives to chemical application to check whether it is possible to avoid chemical use

iii   identify alternative chemicals to do the job

iv   check the possible hazards in each case

v   assess the site of application (is it near habitation, footpath, livestock, inside a building, etc.)

vi   assess method of application

vii   assess necessary precautions and safety equipment

viii   choose the least hazardous alternative chemical method that will fulfil the required purpose

ix   choose appropriate safety equipment

x   re-check decision process.

(Source: British Agrochemicals Association Ltd. "Plain Man's Guide to Pesticides and the C.O.S.H.H. Assessment.")

HEALTH

INTRODUCTION

Winter cereals suffer more seriously from weed, pest and disease problems than Spring sown cereals because they occupy the ground for longer and allow shorter periods of fallow for cleaning operations. The potential losses and the likely costs of control are consequently higher and represent a major threat to the profitability of the enterprise.

WEEDS

Weeds affecting Winter cereals most seriously tend to have some or all of the following characteristics:

> **Autumn germinating**
> **competitive**
> **prolific seed production**
> **seed shed before harvest.**

The most common and damaging are listed in the table below.

Type	Pest organism	Approx.* economic treatment threshold (N° plants/m²)	Approx. potential loss
Grass Weeds	Black-grass Wild-oat Sterile-brome	1 - 2	25 - 30%
	Annual meadow grass	20	5 - 7%
	Couch	50	10 - 15%
Broad-leaved	Cleavers	0.14	30 - 40%
	Mayweeds	5	
	Chickweed	10	
	Speedwells	15 -20	5 - 15%
	Poppy	5	

Notes

* A yield benefit of about 2 - 7% is needed to cover the direct cost of spraying, depending on the expense of the treatment. However, the thresholds include allowance for potential future problems from weed seeds, and extra costs and problems of harvesting, drilling and cleaning.

HEALTH

**   Potential yield losses such as those shown in the table represent severe infestations unlikely to be met within normal commercial practice, unless recommended treatment is neglected. Average losses from annual grass weeds are in the order of 10% and annual broad leaved weeds only 2%.

DISEASES - WHEAT AND BARLEY

Disease	Approx. economic threshold	Approx. potential yield loss%	Likely situation
Leaf diseases			
Yellow rust	2% leaf infection	35% - 40% (less in **barley**)	cool, damp, misty
Septoria tritici	related to specific weather sequence not crop infection level	20% (NOT in **barley**)	prolonged damp or wet period
Powdery mildew	5% leaf infection	10% (30% in **barley**)	warm, humid weather
Rhyncosporium (leaf blotch)		**barley** ONLY	severe in wet, cool weather
Net blotch		**barley** ONLY	severe in wet, humid weather
Brown rust		20%	Warm, humid weather
Root And Stem Base Diseases			
Eyespot	20% tiller infection @ G.S.* 31	10% - 15% (less in **barley**)	long cereal sequence
Take all	No effective chemical treatment	10% - 50% (less in **barley**)	3rd/4th cereal crop light soils
Sharp eyespot	not known	not known	unpredictable
Ear Diseases			
Septoria nodorum	As for *s. tritici*	20% - 25% (NOT in **barley**)	prolonged wet period after ear emergence
Loose smut	not appropriate	not known	undressed seed

* G.S. = Growth stage

HEALTH

Disease	Approx. economic threshold	Approx. potential yield loss%	Likely situation
Barley Yellow Dwarf Virus	presence of aphids in Autumn	20	early sown crop

PESTS

Pest	Approx. economic threshold	Approx. potential yield loss%	Likely situation
Slug	4 slugs per baited trap	20 - 25	warm, moist Autumn/ Winter cloddy seedbed, heavy soil following oilseed rape or peas
Wireworm	$1\frac{1}{2}$ million per hectare		15 - 20 Within 4 years of ploughing long term grass
Frit fly	10% dead hearts	5 - 10	following grass ley or grassy stubble
Wheat bulb fly	$2\frac{1}{2}$ million eggs/ha	25	following early harvested crops, ground bare during July/early August
Aphids	$\frac{2}{3}$ ear infected or 30 per flag leaf	5 - 10	warm dry weather

HEALTH CARE AND HYGIENE

Cultural methods can be a considerable aid to effective control of crop problems.

E.g. preparing a firm seedbed will help prevent slug damage. Use integrated control programmes i.e. a combination of both cultural (variety resistance) and chemical control.

HEALTH

Ploughing	Buries weed seeds and weeds (e.g. 50-60% control of blackgrass)
	Prevents volunteers (reduces carry-over of leaf diseases)
	Buries stubble debris (reduces straw borne disease)
Rotation	Breakcrops avoid build up of soil borne pests and diseases
	Better control of difficult weeds possible
Resistant varieties	Considerable reduction in likelihood of some diseases
Stubble burning	Excellent control of weeds and partial destruction of weed-seeds (however, banned in 1992)
Stubble cultivations	Help to germinate weed and volunteer seeds so that they can be killed
Later drilling	Avoids exposure to high disease pressure (but more susceptible to pest attack e.g. wheat bulb fly) & reduces yield.
Seed dressing	Chemical treatment of seed can reduce the need for some later sprays

LEGAL ASPECTS

Crop protection has become the subject of much recent legislation. Two sets of regulations in particular restrict the freedom of farmers and chemical companies in this area:

F.E.P.A: Food And Environment Protection Act (1985)

F.E.P.A. regulations make the following main demands:

i   that operators of equipment for applying specified chemicals must pass a 2 stage test of knowledge and proficiency before becoming qualified to use the equipment unsupervised

ii that only M.A.F.F. approved chemicals may be used and only at approved rates and times to specified crops

iii that chemicals be stored, handled, applied and disposed of in an approved safe manner

iv that food products be tested and meet strict standards of residue contamination.

OUTSIDER'S GUIDE

HEALTH

C.O.S.H.H.

These regulations place a duty on farmers to make an assessment of risk for each and every use of materials which could harm users or third parties. The procedure involves the following steps:

i   identify the problem

ii   look for non-chemical alternative control

iii If no viable cultural alternative, list possible chemicals

iv check potential hazards of using each material listed

v   check mode and site of application and assess any risks

vi review methods of avoiding risk of contact with chemical

vii choose the chemical with the least possible hazard consistent with effectiveness

viii decide on appropriate protective clothing

ix assess the level of risk

x   plan the application

xi check that staff are aware of safety precautions

xii check health of staff

xiii record operation

xiv review procedure at intervals.

EQUIPMENT, COSTS & WORK RATE

Equipment	Typical cost	Work rate /hour
Crop sprayer		
600 - 800 litres	£2,500 - 10,000	4 ha
1500 - 2000 litres	£6,500 - 18,500	6 ha
Contractors' rates spraying operation	**Cost £/ha**	
Standard (225l/ha)	11.00	
Low Ground Pressure		
Vehicle or High clearance		

HEALTH

HARVESTING

AIM

Harvest cereals when the grains have completely **filled** and **dried** so that the water content is **below 16%**. This moisture % permits safe storage following harvest.

After grain maturity, harvesting requires a **dry period of a day or two** (depending upon wind strength) to dry any water from rain or dew still present on plants which will pass through the harvester.

TIMING CRITERIA

Too early	Too late
high number of green grains	shedding losses likely
drying & storage problems	poorer quality samples
low specific weight	more likely discoloured
difficult to thresh	sprouting grains

Despite the problems of early harvesting, the crop might still be taken early...

Reasons For Harvesting Early

i   Limited drying capacity

ii Allow timely entry of following crop

iii Avoid shedding

iv Prevent drop in Hagberg in Milling Wheat

Visual Assessment

Crop	Straw	Ears
Wheat	mainly light yellow	golden with a proportion able to be snapped off in good conditions
Barley	mainly light yellow	bent over so that very few show across field
Oats	still slightly green	golden with top grains ripe and bottom grains slightly immature left longer and top grains will shed

HARVESTING

Hand Assessment

Grain can be rubbed out easily from the chaff.

Grain too hard to be dented with thumb nail, but not "flinty" (shiny) when cracked open.

Moisture Content

Dry years: Leave until 16% moisture (providing there is no shedding of grains).

Wet years: Harvest when ripe if crop can be dried.

QUALITY CRITERIA

Variety

First harvest those with least resistance to ear loss or shedding of grains.

Market

Feed: Low priority - lowest quality grain.

Milling: In wet years harvest early as this gives a higher Hagberg number for better quality bread .

Malting: Preserve germination ability by timely harvest.

Seed: Harvest before any sprouting risk.

Other factors

Combine settings - ensure properly set and sieves clean to minimise grain losses and damage.

Weather effects - wet grain is difficult to thresh and dry grain is more easily cracked or damaged.

POST HARVEST

Stubble Hygiene

This is the removal of weeds and 'volunteer' cereals (reducing the risk of disease carry over).

Methods:

i   **Cultivations**: Ploughing and/or shallow cultivation. Conditions must be dry. Repeated cultivations necessary.

ii **Herbicides**: Saves time, labour, fuel, machinery costs.

Contact herbicides: Economic to use on annual weeds. These work on contact with the plant, and good plant coverage is needed to be effective.

Systemic herbicides: More effective and usually essential for perennial weeds. The chemical is absorbed into the plant, and moves within it to disrupt plant growth.

Many herbicides now combine systemic and contact action.

Residue Disposal

By incorporation and baling

Effect On	Type of effect	
	Incorporate	Bale
Reducing Pest/Disease	Bad	None
Reducing Slugs	Bad	None
Drainage/Soil Structure	V.Good	Bad
Minimum Cultivations	Bad	None
Following Crop	Bad	None
Nutrient Return	Good	Bad

Burning is now banned due to recent legislation (1989).

STORAGE

For safe storage grain should be kept cool and dry. Generally grain will store safely up to 15°C and 15% moisture.

Other storage options include sealed storage of moist grain or treatment with propionic acid (e.g. "Propcorn") to prevent deterioration. However, grain stored by these methods is suitable only for animal feed.

Pre-cleaning

Passing grain through a machine to remove trash, green material, weed seeds, etc. reduces the moisture content and reduces the drying requirements.

HARVESTING

Drying

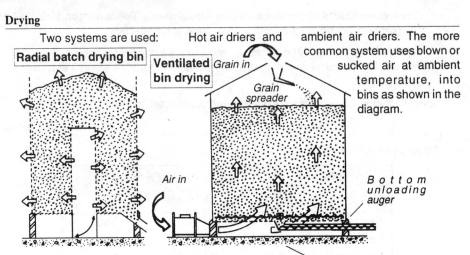

Two systems are used: Hot air driers and   ambient air driers. The more common system uses blown or sucked air at ambient temperature, into bins as shown in the diagram.

Radial batch drying bin

Ventilated bin drying

Grain in

Grain spreader

Air in

Bottom unloading auger

Alternatively, grain may be stored on the floor over air ducts or mesh flooring through which ambient air is pumped.

On-floor driers

Lateral ducts above floor

Lateral ducts below floor

Drying air

Sources Of Damage During Storage

Source of loss	Condition
Mould	Damp grain (above 15% moisture)
Insects	Warm (above 15°C)
Mites	Most conditions except very dry and cold

Safe Storage Life (Wheat)

Moisture Content %	Grain temperature	
	10°C	20°C
17.5	11 weeks	3.5 weeks
15.5	38 weeks	13 weeks

HARVESTING

Store Hygiene

The aim is to exclude insect pests and mites. This requires:

i sound **structure** - no cracks etc. to harbour insects

ii **brush** and vacuum before use

iii **spray appropriate chemical** before use

iv mix **insecticide** with grain if pest problems are likely

v ensure grain is **clean**, **dry** and **cool** before entry

Monitoring And Sampling

Grain can deteriorate quickly so monitor regularly, with many sample points, at varying depths using a grain spear.

i Plot grain temperature and moisture over time - beware a sudden rise

ii Examine samples for pest activity and mould

EQUIPMENT, COSTS AND WORK RATE

Equipment	Typical cost	Work rate/hr
Combine harvester	£50- £70,000	1.5 ha
Grain trailers	£5,000	-
Straw baler (big or high capacity)	£9 - £15,000	1.0 ha
Bale handling equipment	£2,500	-
Straw chopper	£3,500	-
Grain drier (mobile)	£30,000	10 tonnes
Grain store on floor	£50 - 220/tonne store capacity	
Grain movement equipment	£4,500	40 tonnes
Contractors charges	**£**	
Combining	£82.00/ha	
Pick up baling	£0.18/bale	
Combining & carting	£106.25/ha	
Straw chopping	£29.05/ha	

HARVESTING

 ### LEGAL ASPECTS

Storage Pest Control

There is now a compulsory pesticide scheme for all grain. All loads of grain that leave the farm must be accompanied by a Grain Passport. The passport gives details of any post harvest applied pesticides.

Straw And Stubble Burning

Burning has been banned from 1993 due to 1989 legislation.

MAFF survey shows that the area burnt declined 19% between 1990 and 1992. 14.6% of straw was burnt in 1991 compared with 25.3% 1989, 38% 1983.

PERFORMANCE

 KEY ASSESSMENT QUESTIONS

Factors Affecting Yield

i   Soil type

Heavy land	The classic situation for winter wheat. Moisture retentive and fertile soils give good yield and quality when the crop is sown well in good condition.
	Winter barley can also be grown satisfactorily but does not respond so well to the conditions as wheat, and normally fails to reach malting quality. (N% excessive).
Light land	Typically barley land but wheat has invaded land in recent years, previously considered unsuitable. Much lower yield potential, and more liable to take all infections (see ✒)
Medium (loam) soils	Are generally better yielding than either extreme. Grow wheat or barley.
Silty fen soils	Excellent wheat soils but is considered as a breakcrop between more valuable vegetables and potatoes

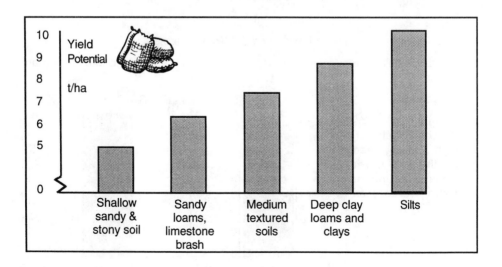

PERFORMANCE

ii Input level

Wheat crops with a potential to produce 8-10 tonnes/ha justify a substantial level of inputs to sustain and protect the yield. However, the converse should also be recognised, crops on low yield sites should be treated proportionally.

Typical variable costs would be:

High	£250/ha
Low	£200/ha

Winter barley inputs would be expected to be lower than wheat, due to lower nutrient requirements and reduced spray cost.

Typical variable cost would be: **£180 - £250/ha.**

iii Drilling date

Late drilling, (November rather than end of September) generally reduces yield, but compensation benefits counteract this effect to some extent, e.g.

| Less disease |
| Less lodging |
| Less weed control problems |

Some late drilled crops yield very well provided conditions at and after drilling are favourable.

iv Variety

Roughly 15% difference between high yielding feed quality and lower yielding milling or malting varieties on the NIAB list.

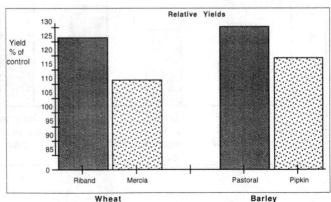

PERFORMANCE

v Disease, weed and pest levels

Varies between situations. Tends to be worse when:

> long sequence of cereals
> minimal cultivated or direct drilled
> poor crop hygiene
> compacted or water logged soil.

FACTORS AFFECTING PRICE

Season

Market price reflects intervention price, but can exceed it in years of good export trade and moderate production level (like 1990).

 Intervention Price For 1994-95 Milling Wheat, Feed Barley, Rye

	Intervention price (£)
November 1994	102.04
May 1995	108.85

Note: Feed wheat can no longer be offered for intervention.

Quality

Milling wheat normally commands a premium over feed which in the 1994/95 season is £15 - £20 per tonne.

Milling oats normally commands a premium over feed which in the 1994/95 season is about £8 per tonne.

Malting barley of the best quality is always in strong demand and receives a premium of up to £25 - 35 per tonne over feed quality. Normally it is sold early in the season. However, due to variety and reduced nitrogen level applied, there is typically a yield penalty from growing malting barley .

Time of sale

Price normally rises after harvest by an amount roughly equating to the cost of storage. Intervention price rises by monthly increments of about £1.13/t/month.

PERFORMANCE

GROSS MARGINS

Typical Average Gross Margins (Inc. area payments of £250/ha)

		Barley	Wheat	Oats
Yield (Tonnes/ha)		6.0	7.25	6.0
Price £/t	Feed	87	90	92.5
	Milling		104	100
	Malting	104		
Output £	Feed	770	900	805
	Milling		925	850
	Malting	811		
Variable costs £	Seed	47.5	45	49
	Fertiliser	65	70	59
	Sprays	87.5	105	55
	Sundries	-	-	5
Total V. cost £ (straw retained)		200	220	168

Gross margin £/ha

	Barley	Wheat	Oats
Feed	570	680	640
Milling		680	685
Malting	570		

Adapted from: J. Nix

FIXED COSTS

Profitable farms manage to minimise fixed costs, and to maximise output from their type of farming system so that fixed costs per unit output are as low as possible.

The figures below are typical levels of fixed costs for a specialist cereal farm. Individual farms will vary in their levels of fixed costs for specific reasons - e.g. new farms will have **rental charges of 40% to 70%** higher than those quoted. Larger farms will tend to have lower fixed costs/hectare.

Mainly cereal farm of 120 - 240 ha

(> 70% land for combinable crops)

Fixed costs:	£ / Hectare
Regular labour	160
Depreciation	95
Repairs, tax and insurance - equipment	50
Fuel and electricity	32
Contract charges - hedging/ditching	20
Land maintenance (fencing, repairs etc).	20
Rent & rates	120
Fees, office expenses	40
TOTAL	**537**

Adapted from: A.B.C.

Average Tenant's Capital

This is the value of investment normally provided by the tenant such as machinery, crops in store and other assets required to run the business.

Mainly cereals farm <200ha	£/ha
Livestock	225
Crops and cultivations	390
Machinery & equipment	575
TOTAL	**1190**

Adapted from: A.B.C.

OUTSIDER'S GUIDE

PERFORMANCE

THE
OUTSIDER'S GUIDE
to
LINSEED

1995 Edition

PRODUCTION

PRODUCTION

Linseed (*Linum usitatissimum*) and flax are the same species. While flax varieties have been selected for straw production and for fibre manufacture, linseed varieties were selected for oil production.

The increasing interest in linseed stems from a variety of factors, not least of which are the levels of subsidy and opportunities for diversification.

Total World Production

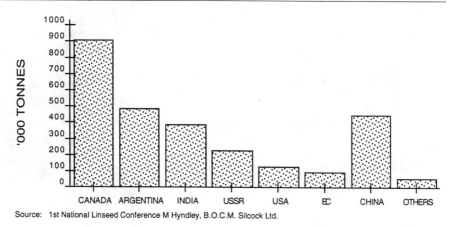

Source: 1st National Linseed Conference M Hyndley, B.O.C.M. Silcock Ltd.

Note: Despite the apparent downward trend, world production has remained relatively constant at around 2 million tonnes for the past 40 years.

Canada and Argentina are the leading exporters. India, CIS, USA and the EU remain net-importers despite significant home production.

PRODUCTION IN THE EU

UK is now the largest producer. In 1993 the UK accounted for 94% of the total EU crop, followed by France and Denmark.

Linseed prefers cool damp conditions therefore is well suited to UK maritime conditions. Southern EU states are too warm and dry to achieve satisfactory linseed yields.

Whilst the EU remains the largest linseed importer, there is considerable scope for expanded production, particularly within the UK with its obvious climatic advantages.

PRODUCTION

UK PRODUCTION/TRENDS AND CYCLES

UK Linseed Area

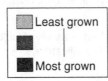

Least grown

|

Most grown

i   58% reduction in area grown in 1994 after very difficult harvest in 1993. Some crops not harvested until late Nov, if at all!

ii   UK average yield is 1.6t/ha very dependent upon the season.

iii   Opportunity to export to other EU countries could mean potential area may expand to 200,000 ha.

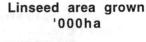

Linseed area grown '000ha

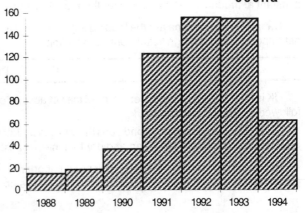

PRODUCTION

UK PRODUCTION

The Agricultural Expansion Programme of 1947 led to a peak of 35,000 ha by 1948, after which, the crop rapidly declined despite Ministry of Agriculture grant aid.

- From 1950 to the early 1970's linseed was considered a "minor crop" in Ministry of Agriculture statistics.

- Following entry to the EU and the introduction of linseed support schemes, the crop increased to 32,000 ha in 1976.

- Disappointing yields in the drought of 1976, coupled with the competition from a rapidly expanding oilseed rape crop again resulted in a reduced acreage.

- During the 1980's the linseed crop has again expanded to 33,700 ha in 1990, this time due to:

  a   improved subsidy arrangements and a higher than average increase in guide price

  b   improved linseed agronomy and increased yield

  c   declining cereal margins, poor yields from other spring crops

  d   introduction of stripper-headers to combines has improved harvester efficiency

  e   growers in 1990 turned to spring sown linseed as a last minute alternative to winter barley crops badly damaged by late Spring frosts.

WHY GROW THIS CROP? - AGRONOMIC BENEFITS

Agronomic benefits	Financial benefits
Can be grown on virtually any soil type	Relatively low variable costs
Good break crop i.e. not susceptible to, and does not act as host to cereal diseases	Price support system
Although herbicide selection is limited, good grass and broad-leaved weed control possible	Good demand within UK and EU only 50% self-sufficient
The following cereal crop should produce a higher yield	Grower contracts readily available from willing merchants
Few pest and disease problems	Possibility of good gross margin on poorer soil typesdue to area subsidy
Seed capsules not prone to shatter unless harvest delayed as in the wet Autumn of 1992.	No specialist machinery required with the possible exception of a stripper header, unless contractor used.

PRODUCTION

FACTORS AFFECTING PROFITABILITY

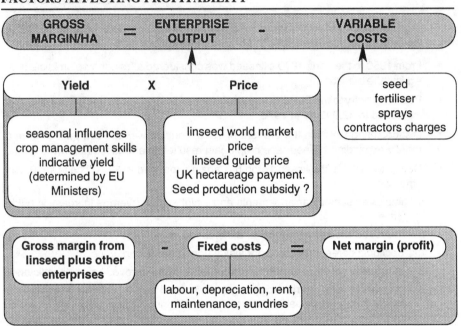

| GROSS MARGIN/HA | = | ENTERPRISE OUTPUT | − | VARIABLE COSTS |

Yield X **Price**

seed
fertiliser
sprays
contractors charges

seasonal influences
crop management skills
indicative yield
(determined by EU
Ministers)

linseed world market
price
linseed guide price
UK hectareage payment.
Seed production subsidy ?

| Gross margin from linseed plus other enterprises | − | Fixed costs | = | Net margin (profit) |

labour, depreciation, rent,
maintenance, sundries

 ### KEY ASSESSMENT QUESTIONS

Yield tonnes/ha	1.75	
Prices @ £/t	120	(prone to wide fluctuations)
Output £/ha	210	
Subsidy £	480	
Total	**690**	
Variable costs	175	
Gross margin	**515**	
@ Oil content std	38%	
Moisture content	9%	
Admixture	0%	

MARKETING

MARKETING

Main Products

Oil

The main product is oil as linseed has an oil content of approximately 38-40%. This oil is used as a technical/industrial oil rather than edible oil.

Expelled oil used for:

paints, putty, wood preservatives, varnishes, printing ink	linseed oil has good sticking and drying properties. Forms a durable film covering on exposure to air.
linoleum/lino manufacture and lubricants	expanding industrial floor covering market.

Livestock feeds

Remaining residue (high in protein) utilised in livestock feeds, often in the form of "expeller-cake". Limited inclusion rates unfortunately due to low methionine & lysine amino acid levels.

Secondary Uses

Bird seed.

Boiled whole as an equine feed.

Human consumption (limited)

Possible future use for linseed straw in fibre products, particle board horticultural media products.

UK AND EUROPEAN IMPORTS AND EXPORTS

Imports ('000 t)

	1986/87	1987/88	1988/89	1989/90	1990/91
Into UK	39	29	13	10	12
Into Europe	544	437	232	325	302

Source: OILWORLD September 1991

Note: 1991/2 the UK is no longer a net importer.

MARKETING

Notes on imports and exports.

i low yields in N. America and Canada in 1988 resulted in high world prices and reduced European imports

ii large acreages and good yields in Canada in 1990 resulted in lower prices

iii the EU remains the largest linseed importer in the world

iv clearly, considerable scope exists in the UK to supply both our domestic linseed requirements and to replace a proportion of European imports

v crushers may look to secure supplies up to 18 months in advance. It may be possible therefore to sell the crop before it is even sown! Considerable premiums may be possible over the spot price at harvest

 LINSEED QUALITY STANDARDS

Crushing Standards		
Moisture content	Basis 9%	
Admixture	Basis 0%	} deductions for each 1% below these standards
Oil content	Basis 38%	
Seed Standard		
Purity	99% minimum	
Germination	85% minimum	
Disease e.g.	*Botrytis* spp	5% maximum
	Alternaria spp *Fusarium* spp *Phoma exigua* *Colletotrichum*	} + 5% maximum in 150 g sample
Other plant species Wild Oat Blackgrass	15 seeds maximum Nil 4 seeds maximum	
Source: International Seed Producers 1991, revised 1992		

MARKETING

VARIETY CHOICE

Consider the following:

i Seed yield - influences output slightly

ii Oil content

iii Lodging resistance (early lodging can greatly reduce yields if crop does not recover)

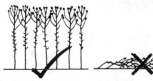

iv Maturity (early maturing varieties preferred under UK conditions for heavier and later soil types, but lighter & earlier soils can grow later maturing varieties). Due to difficult harvests in '92 & '93 growers will look for earlier maturing types in future.

v Seed size - Belgium for example demands large seeded types will also affect seed rate.

vi Disease resistance (particularly Botrytis) - may save fungicide costs later.

Examples

Variety	Features
Antares	Remains a popular linseed variety. But moderately stiff straw, medium maturity and average straw length. Performs well in drought conditions. Only average yield.
Blue Chip	Highest seed yield at 109% of control, and highest oil content at 41.0%. But poor standing power and very late to mature.
Norlin	The earliest variety to mature but lower yielding. Surprisingly slow to flower.
Barbara	Joint highest yielding variety in NIAB trials, with good oil content. Earlier than Blue chip.
Mikael	Average yield, very short stem, early to flower but similar maturity as Antares.

Note: little independent variety assessment available at present. The NIAB list is only a descriptive list, and not a recommended list.

ENVIRONMENT

CLIMATE

Linseed is well suited to the UK's cool moist, maritime climate. Dry Augusts encourage even maturity and dry Septembers enable— easier harvesting.

Linseed is less susceptible to drought than other Spring sown crops. Every effort should be made to encourage rapid tap root growth within the top 60 cm of soil, in order to help take up sufficient moisture.

Regular moisture during the growing season is an advantage.

Dry, sunny ripening and harvesting conditions are essential. SE Counties ideal, Northern Counties and Scotland are often too moist during crucial harvesting period.

Irrigation is usually unnecessary and unlikely to be economic.

SOILS

Well structured, reasonably water retentive soils are ideal. Linseed can perform surprisingly well on "less-productive" soils when area subsidy is taken into account.

Light, sandy soils are prone to drought.

Heavy soils are likely to lead to establishment difficulties and delayed maturity.

pH

Linseed is suited to a range of pH above 6.0.

Lime if pH is significantly less than 6.5.

DRAINAGE

Linseed does not possess a vigorous rooting system, therefore avoid soils prone to water logging.

TYPICAL ROTATIONS

Linseed is unrelated to other farm crops and can easily be included in most arable rotations.

The minimum rotation is 1 in 5 years. Special care must be taken when including peas and beans in a linseed rotation to allow a similar gap of 5 years between linseed and peas and beans to avoid the build up of soil-borne Sclerotinia.

OUTSIDER'S GUIDE

ENVIRONMENT

Resistance to wire-worm can be a valuable feature following long term grass.

Should not be grown in a rotation with vining peas because of volunteer linseed capsules contaminating the crop.

Linseed can be grown after root crops e.g. late harvested potatoes and beet, providing a "double-break". High grade cereal seed crops could then be grown. But beware compaction following late harvested root crops.

Example rotation: 1 in 5 rotation

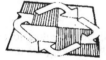

Year		
	1	Winter wheat
	2	Linseed
	3	Set-aside
	4	Winter barley
	5	Oilseed rape

TYPICAL CULTIVATIONS

Successful establishment is the key to a high yielding crop.

Aims

- **Fine** soil particle size for good seed/soil contact. Autumn plough heavy soils to produce maximum weathering effect.

Autumn plough   Frost mould by spring

- **Consolidate** by rolling to conserve moisture. Avoid rolling after drilling to avoid soil-capping on susceptible soils. If rolling post-emergence, allow adequate recovery time before applying herbicides.

- **Level** to ensure even drilling depth. Linseed will emerge unevenly if drilled any deeper than 2.5 cm. Drilling too shallow, can reduce establishment by drought.

- **Compaction** greatly reduces yield potential. Remove any compaction

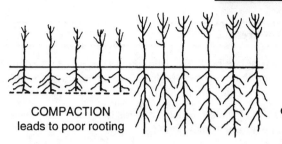

NO COMPACTION
enables good tap root
penetration

COMPACTION
leads to poor rooting

before ploughing and avoid unnecessary wheelings over the seedbed.

Note: Aim for a plant population of about 500-600/m². As seed accounts for 45% of variable costs, seed rates should be as accurate as possible. Drills should be accurately calibrated before sowing and the thousand grain weight must be known as this can vary greatly according to variety. Aim for a seed rate of 600-700 seeds/m².

% Establishment can be as low as 40%.

Narrow 9 - 12 cm rows are preferred.

Typical Cultivation Sequence And Costs

Cultivation	Contractors charge £/ha
Subsoil (if necessary: 450mm deep,1.2m centres)	54.11
Plough	30.20
Springtime cultivations x 2	18.55
Drill seed	18.55
Roll (ribbed roller type, pre or post drilling or both)	£14.85

Source: A.B.C.

C.O.S.H.H. (Control of Substances Hazardous to Health)

Take all necessary precautions particularly in relation to:

pesticide use (protect both the operator and the environment)

dust (avoid any unnecessary exposure - see ✎ for details)

Note: Bulk linseed behaves as a liquid rather than a solid therefore take special care, you can drown in linseed!

ENVIRONMENT

NSA'S (Nitrate Sensitive Areas)

Advantage   As linseed requires only 75kg Nitrogen/ha there is a reduced leaching risk. Also, the deep tap root tends to take up residual nitrogen from deeper within the soil profile.

Disadvantage Linseed is Spring drilled. Soluble nitrates remaining after the previous crop may leach over the Winter period.

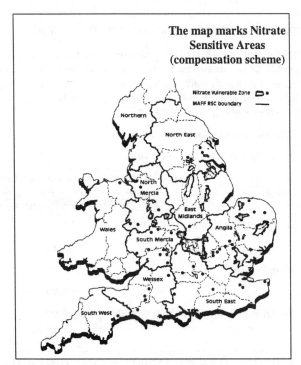

The map marks Nitrate Sensitive Areas (compensation scheme)

Nitrate Vulnerable Zone
MAFF RSC boundary

Northern
North East
North Mercia
East Midlands
Wales
Anglia
South Mercia
Wessex
South East
South West

Influence Of Windbreak

Even when fully mature, linseed is relatively robust and would not benefit greatly from wind protection, although some protection at the seedling stage would be an advantage.

Nearness to hedges etc. can in fact be a disadvantage as the shading effect leads to uneven maturity. Pests such as pigeons, rabbits, aphids, bugs, thrips and flea beetle are all encouraged by hedges and woods.

GROWTH STAGES

PRODUCTION CYCLE

Ploughing

DEC · JAN · NOV · OCT · FEB · MAR · SEPT · APR · AUG · MAY · JULY · JUNE

Prepare fine, firm seedbed

Apply basal N, P, K.

Dry to below 9%M.C.

Drill crop

Harvest

Post-emergence weed control

Desiccation

Possible N top dressing

Possible flea beetle control

Flowering - mainly self pollinating

LINSEED GROWTH STAGES

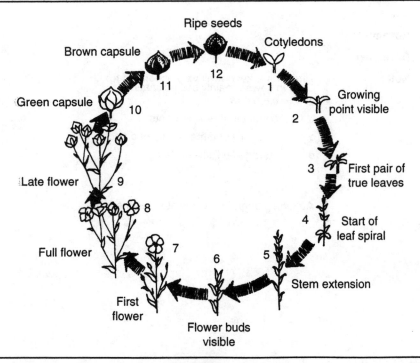

Ripe seeds

Brown capsule

Cotyledons

11 12 1

Green capsule 10

Growing point visible 2

3 First pair of true leaves

Late flower 9

4 Start of leaf spiral

8

Full flower

7 6 5

Stem extension

First flower

Flower buds visible

GROWTH STAGES

 Crop Calendar

January

February

March/April   Prepare seedbed, fine and firm. Drill crop. Apply seedbed (basal) fertiliser, N, P and K.

April/May   Post-emergence weed control. Possibly top-dress with Nitrogen. Possible flea beetle control.

Mid June

July

August/September

Pre-harvest treatment e.g. desiccation followed by harvest. Dry crop to below 9% moisture. Bulk linseed will deteriorate rapidly over 9% moisture content (M.C.)

October

November

December

Note: } Time of marketing will vary according to:
Crop in flower, mainly self pollinating.

    a   cash flow

    b   contractual requirements

    c   level of world market linseed price

    d   storage facilities on-farm

} Autumn plough for over-winter weathering.

GROWTH STAGES

Growth stage	Description	Typical operation/ comments
Establishment Pre-emergence G.S. 1 Crop drilled late March, early April		Pre-emergence Seedbed fertiliser applied (Basal)
G.S. 2	*Cotyledon*	
G.S. 3	*Growing point emerged*	
G.S. 4	*First pair of true leaves unfolded*	Post-emergence herbicides can be applied from this G.S. onwards
G.S. 5	*Third pair of true leaves unfolded*	Post-emergence rolling can be carried out at this stage but allow an adequate healing period between rolling and herbicide application

GROWTH STAGES

Growth stage	Description	Typical operation/comments
G.S. 6	*Stem extension*	Final growth stage for most herbicides. Possibly apply a plant growth regulator
G.S. 7 (early June)	*Flower buds visible. Rapid stem extension continues*	
G.S. 8 (mid June)	*First flowers produced and upper plant branches.*	Pale blue flowers. Petals produced and shed daily
G.S. 9	*Full flower: branching continues. Capsules start to form*	Possibly apply fungicide against Botrytis
G.S. 10	*Late flowering*	
G.S. 11	*Capsules green, seed white, leaves yellowing*	Consider "Roundup" (Glyphosate) application as a pre-harvest treatment towards the end of this G.S
G.S. 12	*Brown capsules, seeds light brown. Leaves start to senesce. Seeds rattle within the capsule. Seeds now darker brown in colour*	Apply a pre-harvest desiccant e.g. Reglone (Diquat). Variety Beryl has a light yellow seed colour!
HARVEST (late August/ early September)		Pre harvest treatment essential to ensure a successful and timely harvest

NUTRITION

Nitrogen (N) kg/ha

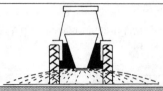

Soil Nitrogen Index (kg/ha)			
Previous crop type			
	0	**1**	**2**
Seedbed	50	40	nil
Top-dressing	30	nil	nil
Total	80	nil	nil

Source: M.A.F.F. Fertiliser Recommendations (mineral soils)

Note:

1.   For crops drilled after mid April, apply all N in the seedbed.

2.   On shallow soils over chalk, trial evidence would suggest increasing N rates up to 100kg/ha, but beware - see note 3.

3.   Excessive N applications lead to increased lodging, delayed flowering and harvesting difficulties.

4.   Top-dress N at growth stage 3 (first pair of true leaves unfolded).

Phosphate And Potash

Linseed is rarely responsive to P and K and 40-50 kg/ha is usually adequate to maintain soil fertility. For P and K indices above 3, additional P and K is not required.

Growers should avoid combine drilling of seed and fertiliser which can lead to reduced establishment. Instead, the fertiliser should be applied during seedbed preparation.

OUTSIDER'S GUIDE

NUTRITION

Lime

pH - ideally pH 6.5.

linseed is not acid tolerant

linseed appears to perform particularly well on high pH chalk and limestone i.e. calcareous soils, above pH 7.0

Growth Regulators

The use of growth regulators in combination with increased nitrogen levels in order to promote yield, is currently under investigation.

For the moment, excessive lodging can usually be prevented by:

correct level of Nitrogen use

sensible variety choice

avoiding excessive plant populations.

NUTRIENT DEFICIENCY SYMPTOMS

Major Nutrient Deficiency Symptoms

Nutrient	Deficiency symptoms
Nitrogen (N)	Small leaf area. Leaves light green to yellow in colour. Few side branches bearing capsules
	Erect growth habit
	Plants ripen prematurely with reduced yield
	Deficient plants often found on headlands where compaction leads to poor rooting
	Symptoms often confused with water-logging
Phosphate (P)	Stunting
	Leaves a darker green in colour
	Premature leaf death, particularly the lower leaves
Potash (K)	Very similar to phosphate deficiency with the addition of necrotic leaf tips
	Possibly increased lodging especially where high N rates have been applied

Micro Nutrients

Nutrient	Background	Deficiency symptoms/control
Magnesium (Mg)	An intermediate or secondary element. Forms part of the chlorophyll molecule therefore involved in photosynthesis. Most UK soils have adequate reserves	More likely in acid soils & in cold, wet, conditions. Symptoms include stunting & inter-veinal yellowing. Apply Kieserite (16% Mg) before linseed or apply a foliar Mg spray
Boron (B)	Linseed is moderately susceptible to Boron deficiency. Involved in sugar translocation, seed set and development	Easily leached therefore more likely on light, sandy soils. Becomes less available at pH levels above 7.0 Chlorotic younger leaves, thickened stems and twisted growing point may eventually die. Apply foliar Boron e.g. "Solubor"
Manganese (Mn)	Again involved in photosynthesis and oxygen formation	Deficiency encouraged by over liming or naturally high pH soils. Younger leaves have a mottled, chlorotic appearance. Leaf analysis essential to confirm deficiency. Apply Manganese Sulphate and wetter as soon as symptoms appear

Typical Fertiliser Costs

		£/tonne		
Straights	Urea 46% N	105	-	120
	34.5% N e.g. "Nitram"	95	-	110
	Muriate of Potash (60% K)	100	-	115
	Triplesuperphosphate (46% P)	115	-	125
	Kieserite (16% Mg)	105	-	112
	Ground limestone (spread)	14	-	22

Source: A.B.C.

NUTRITION

Compounds	N	P	K	£/tonne		
Analysis %	17	17	17	120	-	135
	20	10	10	112	-	122
	20	5	15	112	-	122

Fertilising Equipment And Costs

	£		
Mounted spinner type 210 - 2500 litres hopper	600	-	5500
Trailed spinner type 1500 - 5000 litres hopper	2750	-	10500
" " " 6000 - 10000 litres hopper	9500	-	15000
Pneumatic spreaders mounted 12m	4000	-	8000
" " " 12 - 21m	4500	-	26000
" " trailed 12 - 20m	8000	-	20000

Source: A.B.C.

Typical Contractors Charges

	£/ha
Ploughing	30.20
Sub-soiling	54.11
Power harrowing	29.65
Fertiliser application	8.90
Gang rolling	14.85
Drilling	18.55
Pesticide application	9.90
Harvesting	118.60
Drying to 8%moisture content from 20% MC	16.75-17.25/t
12% MC	9.25-9.75/t

Source: A.B.C.

Note: high drying costs in relation to relatively low value crop (£/t).

OUTSIDER'S GUIDE

Weeds And Weed control

An effective weed control strategy is essential for a number of reasons:

   i   upright growth habit and small leaf area makes linseed a poor competitor.

   ii   fine, firm seedbed to encourage rapid linseed establishment also favours both grass and broad leaved weeds.

   iii weedy crops mature slowly and unevenly making harvesting more difficult.

   iv   the presence of green material will slow down drying.

Linseed - The Problem Weeds

Annual Broad Leaved Weeds (A.B.L.W.) :
Knotgrass
Redshank
Pale Persicaria
Fat Hen
Charlock
Cleavers
Thistles
Chickweed
Common Poppy
Runch

} Spring germinating polygonums

Knotgrass seedling

Annual Grass Weeds (A.G.W.) :
Volunteer Cereals
Wild Oats
Blackgrass
Couch
Annual Meadow Grass

Wild oats

OUTSIDER'S GUIDE

HEALTH

Herbicide Selection

Due to the relatively limited EU linseed crop, and the great expense and delay in introducing new pesticides in the UK, few herbicides are currently recommended for use.

Linseed Herbicides

Herbicide & manufacturer	Active ingredient	Comments
Annual Broad-Leaved Weeds (A.B.L.W.)		
Treflan (Dow Elanco)	Trifluralin	Applied pre-drilling. Cheap good spectrum of weed control. Follow up treatment may be necessary
Basagran (B.A.S.F.)	Bentazone	Post-emergence treatment. Good crop safety. Excellent cleaver control. Often used in mixtures with Vindex.
Dow Shield (Dow Elanco)	Chlorpyralid	Specific thistle control. Often tank-mixed with Basagran
Vindex (Dow Elanco)	Clopyralid + Bromoxynil	Post-emergence before flowering
Ally (Du-Pont)	Metsulfuron -methyl	Contact & Residual B/L weed control. Good on volunteer potatoes.
Annual Grass Weeds (A.G.W.)		
Avadex BW (Monsanto)	Triallate	Excellent blackgrass, wild oats and meadow grass. Applied pre-drilling
Checkmate (Rhone Poulenc)	Sethoxydim	Good grassweed and volunteer cereal control. Sterile Brome, Ryegrass and couch also controlled. No annual meadow grass control. Post emergence
Hoegrass (Agrevo)	Diclopfop-Methyl	Effectiveness improved by competitive crop and cool, moist, conditions

Diseases And Disease Control

Few diseases are of any economic significance in linseed. However, as our understanding of the crop improves and the area increases, fungicide use is likely to increase.

Fungicidal seed treatments e.g. Prelude 20 LF (Prochloraz) are in common use. Fungicides applied to the growing crop are aimed at prevention rather than cure and should therefore be applied before the onset of disease.

Alternaria	Encouraged by cool, moist, conditions. The disease is seed borne therefore effectively controlled at seedling and young plant stage by seed dressing e.g. Iprodione (Rovral)
Mildew	Powdery mildew has been observed on crops in hot, dry, seasons but it is thought to be of little economic importance at present
Botrytis	Both air and seed borne. Encouraged by warm, moist, conditions, dense crops and high nitrogen rates. Fallen petals, trapped within the crop canopy form an ideal micro-climate for the disease control e.g. Rovral
Sclerotinia	Sclerotia present in the seed sample is the usual source. Largely contained by adopting sensible rotation. Not yet a significant problem in the UK but it does threaten to be.

Note - Linseed crops grown for seed certification must be protected against disease. It is recommended that seed crops be treated with a post-flowering fungicide against Alternaria and Botrytis.

Pest And Disease Control

Few pests are of any economic significance in linseed.

Pigeons and Rabbits	Grazing damage leads to secondary branching, late maturity and reduced yields.
Flea Beetle	Eat holes in cotyledons and seedling stems. A more significant pest in late sown crops. Control using HCH spray e.g. Gammacol. Sometimes worth controlling in dry, Springs
Thrips, Leafhoppers and Capsid Bugs	Damage crops around field boundaries resulting in delayed maturity. Control e.g. Decis
Slugs	No damage to linseed crops. Linseed crops removing moisture can in fact reduce slug populations

OUTSIDER'S GUIDE

LEGAL REQUIREMENTS

C.O.S.H.H. (Control Of Substances Hazardous To Health)

Legislation designed primarily to protect employees in all industries.

Hazardous substances include pesticides and harmful dusts.

Before selecting a pesticide, growers should assess the various alternatives and select the product with the least possible risk to an employee.

Employers should also ensure drying sheds etc. are as free as possible from dust and minimise employees exposure to such dusty conditions.

Warn staff about the dangers of drowning in Linseed.

F.E.P.A. (Food And Environmental Protection Act)

Legislation designed to protect both the sprayer operator and the environment as a whole.

Spray operators must in future be certified i.e. prove they are competent in the safe use of sprays and sprayers.

Includes guidance on the safe disposal of spray washings, minimising spray drift etc.

 Spray Equipment And Costs

Sprayers		£
Mounted 600 - 800 litres	12 - 18 m	1,500 - 10,000
" 800 - 1500 litres	12 - 24 m	3,500 - 19,000
Trailed 500 - 2500 litres	12 - 24 m	5,500 - 21,500
" 3000 - 4100 litres	18 - 36 m	14,500 - 44,000
Air Assisted mn'td 500 - 1,000litres	12m	5,000 - 12,000
Self propelled 2500 - 6800 litres	18 - 36 m	38,000 - 82,000

Source A.B.C.

Note

i   Prices quoted before discount

ii   Spray equipment frequently leased

Contractors Charges (excluding pesticides)

Standard spraying 225 1/ha £9.90/ha

HARVESTING

Aims

Try to ensure:

maximum seed harvest

minimum admixture i.e. trash

minimum seed loss. Lost/shed seed could become volunteers in subsequent crops.

many growers now using contractors with stripper headers on their combine

Timing Criteria

Harvesting is usually late August to late September. The crop ripens from the top down, taking on a brown appearance. Ripe seeds are plump and "rattle within the seed capsule". The amount of seed shed from the capsule is normally very little.

From the outset, the crop should be encouraged to mature by September to allow a trouble free harvest and the timely establishment of the following crop.

Unfortunately, the seed capsules are mature for harvesting before the stems have dried out, necessitating a pre-harvest treatment.

Pre-Harvest Treatment Options

1 **Desiccation with Diquat "Reglone"**

Apply when 95% of the seed capsules are brown and rattle. Direct combining can then take place 7-14 days after application. Ensure the Diquat penetrates well into the canopy to desiccate the green stems. Higher water rates essential.

2 **Desiccation with Challenge (Glufosinate-ammonium)**

Spray when the majority (over 50%) of the seed capsules are brown. Allow upto 21 days from application to harvest.

3 **Direct combining**

Direct combining is possible under dry conditions.

Note that the vast majority of growers adopt option 1.

HARVESTING

Quality Criteria

Moisture content - linseed can be successfully harvested up to 15% M.C. and often above. Ideally, it should be harvested at or just below 9% M.C. to avoid drying costs!

Admixture - ensure correct combine setting to avoid unwanted contamination with broken seed capsules, trash etc.

Post-Harvest Crop Care

Linseed will deteriorate rapidly at moisture contents above 9%.

Drying Systems

On floor systems	are suitable provided laterals are closely spaced and crop depth is kept below 750 mm because of the substantial airflow resistance through linseed
Continuous flow driers	again satisfactory provided temperature is kept below 65°C to prevent oil seeping from the seed

Note:

i   Linseed flows particularly easily, behaving as a liquid rather than a solid. Seed loss can easily therefore occur through holes in combines, trailers, conveyors or anything in which it is contained.

ii Do not walk on stored linseed, you can drown!

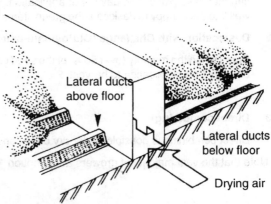

Lateral ducts above floor

Lateral ducts below floor

Drying air

Storage Management Key Points

If necessary, dry linseed as soon as possible.

Avoid temperatures above 65°C, 50°C for seedcrops to protect germination.

Avoid seed leakage.

Take any necessary safety precautions.

Take into account air relative humidity (RH) when drying, it can save considerable costs e.g.:

Linseed Moisture Content %	8	8.5	9*	10	11	12
Air Relative Humidity %	55	60	65	70	75	80

*Contracted moisture content

Ambient air with a RH of 65% or less can be used, without heating, to dry linseed down to the required 9% moisture.

Straw (Crop Residue) Disposal

Straw can be chopped, incorporated or baled. The high calorific value of linseed straw makes it particularly well suited to straw burning boilers.

HARVESTING

EQUIPMENT, COSTS AND CHARGES

	Typical cost £
Harvesting equipment	
Self propelled conventional combines:	
3.1 - 3.6 m (90 - 125 hp)	39,000 - 62,500
3.6 - 4.9 m (100 - 1500 hp)	50,000 - 70,000
Stripper header (well suited to linseed) to fit to a conventional harvester (3.6 - 6.0m)	14,000 - 17,500
Contractors charges	
Direct Combining	118.60/ha
Drying linseed down to 8% moisture from 20%	16.75 - 17.25/t
Drying linseed down to 8% moisture from 12%	9.25 - 9.75/t
Storage per week	0.20 - 0.30/t
Storage costs	
Continuous flow drier 10 - 40 tonnes per hour, cost per tonne of hourly rate.	1,400 - 2,350
Automated batch drier, cost per tonne of hourly rate	2,250 - 3,000
Grain storage (including all services and equipment)	
On floor, no drying capacity	55 - 80/t
On floor, with drier, ducts & laterals	118 - 135/t
Indoor bins, including drying, new building	150 - 175/t
Bins, outdoor, free-standing, ventilated	100 - 125/t

Source: A.B.C.

TYPICAL GROSS MARGIN

	£/ha
Output	
Yield: 1.75 t/ha at £120	210
Area aid subsidy*	480
Total return	690
Variable costs	
Seed	80
Fertilizer	33
Chemicals	62
Total variable costs	175
Gross margin	**515**

Source: *Nix

Physical Performance - Yield By Area

Region	1990 t/ha	1991 t/ha
Scotland	1.33	1.23
Northern	1.89	1.69
Midlands & Western	1.71	1.89
Eastern	1.82	1.78
South East	1.92	1.77
Wales	2.39	1.72
South West	1.83	1.80
Average yield (t/ha)	**1.84**	**1.70**

Ref: Intervention Board

PERFORMANCE

Gross Margin Comparison

Crop	Output t/ha X £/t	Area Aid (Estimate)	Var Costs £/ha	Gross Margin £/ha
Winter wheat	7.25t @ £90	250	220	680
Winter barley	6.0t @ £89	250	200	570
Winter O.S.R.	3.0t @ £150	405	200	665
Dried peas	3.7t @ £95	360	215	495
Winter beans	3.6t @ £87.50	360	130	545
Linseed	1.75t @ £120	481	175	515

Source: A.B.C.

Note:

Gross Margins can vary considerably, particularly according to yields and price/tonne. Linseed can give a similar return as many other break crops.

INDUSTRIAL LINSEED

Linseed for non food use may be grown on set-aside land. Growers must have a signed contract with a first processor before sowing the crop.

The full set-aside payments will be made but no other susidy can be claimed from the EU. 1994 there was was around 14,750ha of linseed grown on set-aside land.

GROSS MARGIN	£/ha
Output 1.75£/ha @£120	210
Set-aside payment	315
Variable Costs	155
Gross Margin	370

OUTSIDER'S GUIDE

FIXED COSTS

Fixed costs are all the costs of a farm business that can not be allocated to individual enterprises as are variable costs. The figures below are approximate being intended for budget preparation. They show the relative fixed costs associated with different farm systems and farm sizes.

Typical Fixed Costs

Farm category	Fixed costs £ha
Mainly cereals up to 120 ha	577
Mainly cereals 120 to 240 ha	537*
Intensive arable up to 100 ha	918
Intensive arable 100 to 200 ha	750

Fixed Cost Components

	*120 - 240 ha
Labour	160
Depreciation	95
Repairs, tax, insurance	50
Fuel and electricity	32
General contract	20
Rent and rates	120
Land maintenance	20
Fixed cost sundries	40
Total fixed costs	**537**

Source A.B.C.

Note:

Fixed costs vary considerably according to circumstances of the farm especially whether it is owned or rented. Fixed costs quoted in the previous table are particularly comprehensive and are therefore likely to be on the high side.

PERFORMANCE

Cost Categories

Labour	includes all full time labour and an estimated value of manual work carried out by the farmer and his family, plus general family labour
Depreciation	calculated on a replacement cost basis
Contract	used for general work only such as hedging or ditching
Rent	actual or rental value including imputed rent on the net costs of improvements
Land maintenance	traditional tenant's repairs plus landlord type repairs carried out by tenants under a full repairing tenancy
Sundries	overheads of the business such as insurance, professional fees, office and telephone, subscriptions etc. but excluding interest charges.

THE
OUTSIDER'S GUIDE
to
OILSEED RAPE

1995 Edition

PRODUCTION

TOTAL PRODUCTION (WORLD)

World production of oilseeds, (including oilseed rape) is approximately 170 million tonnes, of which about 50% is soya. The EU produces approximately 515 m tonnes of oilseed rape. Other major oil sources include palm oil, olive oil, sunflower oil and ground nut oil.

Within the EU, the UK is in third place in the production league behind France and Germany. It should be noted that French rape production is declining in favour of sunflowers.

EEU OILSEED RAPE PRODUCTION

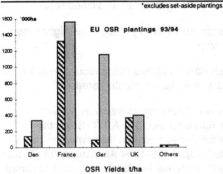

*excludes set-aside plantings.

France, Germany, the UK and Denmark are the major oilseed rape producers in the EU.

The chart shows the area of oilseed rape grown in the EU 12.

The total 1994 crop is estimated to be 610,000ha above the EU maximum guaranteed area of 3.371 million hectares.

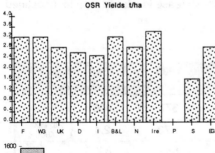

Following talks between the EU and the USA a revised MGA (maximum guaranteed area) will come into effect from 1995 of 5,309,000ha total oilseeds including sunflowers. For every 1% over production, compensatory payments are reduced by 1%. The UK share of the MGA is 327,000ha rising to 339,000ha in 1995 Agreement. (At the time writing, there is likely to be a 7-14% penalty payment for UK growers.)

Source of charts: The N.F.U. "Inside Track"

UK RAPE PRODUCTION

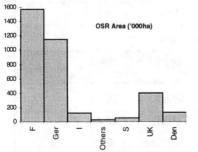

After peaking at 445,000ha in 1991, the UK oilseed rape acreage declined and has now increased again to 405,900ha. Also UK oilseed for industrial uses on set-aside land, is currently estimated to account for about 91,720ha.

OUTSIDER'S GUIDE

PRODUCTION

Production Trends

1970 - 1985 A period of rapid expansion due to:

* the US embargo on soya exports to Europe encouraged home production
* the introduction of a price support scheme (actually a crushers subsidy)
* the fact that oilseed rape was a suitable break crop for heavy land farmers

1986 - 1988 Acreage declined due to:

* the poor yields in 1985
* a growing uncertainty over continuation of EU financial support for the crop
* low prices
* uncertainty over the introduction of lower yielding double low oilseed rape

1988 - 1989 Expansion once more in acreage terms brought about by higher rape prices, and renewed confidence in the crop.

1991 - 1992 MAFF estimate the 1992 OSR harvest at 969,000t a reduction of 13.1% due to a combination of lower yield and a reduction in planted area.

1992 - 1993 Dramatic reduction in area sown. Down by as much as 40% in some areas due to the crops' uncertain future following G.A.T.T. Since the introduction of set-aside, growers have tended to maintain their wheat acreage but reduce their OSR and barley crop. 1993-1994 An increase of 8% due to expansion of spring acreage (Also 84% increase in oilseed rape for undefined use.)

Production Statistics

Survey of production	1992	1993	1994 *excludes set-aside oilseeds	
Area ('000 hectares)	421	377	406	
Average yield (t/ha)	2.68	2.73	2.4	2.82 winter 2.00 spring
Production ('000t)	969	859	800	

Source: N.F.U. "Inside Track"

Breakdown of Harvest Area	1992	1993	1994
Autumn sown	83.2%	66.8%	56.6%
Spring Sown	16.8%*	33.2%	43.4%
Double Low Varieties	93%**	92%	96%

* The rapid increase in spring O.S.R can be attributed to 2 factors:-

1   The failure of winter sown crops. (In Autumn 1991 due to dry conditions and poor establishment. In Autumn 1993 due to wet conditions reduced winter cereal drilling).

2   The acreage subsidy for Winter and Spring rape is identical, and because the Spring crop is cheaper to grow, it could be more profitable.

** The decline in double low varieties is due to the increase in single low, high erucic acid varieties grown for industrial uses. Single lows can be grown on set-aside land. The UK single low area for 1992 is estimated at 24,000ha. Unfortunately, Europe is now self sufficient in the crop unless alternative industrial uses can be found. Single low crops should be grown at least 100metres away from low crops to prevent cross pollination.

EU Position

Latest estimates for the 1994 harvest suggest a crop of 406 thousand hectares which will trigger an MGA (Maximum Guaranteed Area) price cut.

Yield Variation Amongst Growers

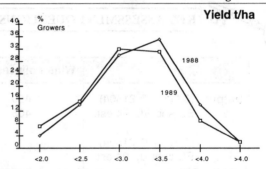

WHY CHOOSE OILSEED RAPE AS A COMBINABLE BREAK CROP?

- ☞ Good gross margin, comparable with Winter wheat
- ☞ Utilises existing equipment e.g. drill and combine
- ☞ Good grass weed control possible within oilseed rape crops
- ☞ Good break from increasing wheat diseases
- ☞ Good entry for Winter wheat:

*weed and disease break	*early wheat establishment possible
*residual N left over in stubble debris	*improved soil structure. Oilseed rape has a deep tap root.

PRODUCTION

For these reasons, the area of oilseed rape has tended to increase over recent years, but due to the uncertainty regarding EU subsidies the 1993 area grown was down.

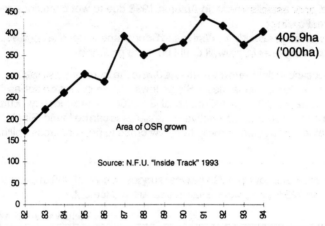

405.9ha
('000ha)

Area of OSR grown

Source: N.F.U. "Inside Track" 1993

KEY ASSESSMENT QUESTIONS

		Winter oilseed rape	Spring oilseed rape
Output	(3.0t/ha @ £150/t)	450	
	EC subsidy '94 est.	405	
	(2.1t/ha @ £150/t)		286
	EC subsidy '94 est.		405
Total variable costs (£/ha)		200	145
Gross margin (£/ha)		**655**	**575**

Source: J. Nix 1994

1992 Subsidy Change

The switch from tonnage to area (acreage) subsidy applied from 1992 harvest. The crop will then be traded at world market prices. High inputs producing only modest yield improvements will no longer be cost-effective. Variable costs of production will almost certainly be reduced, but the effect upon yield is uncertain.

FACTORS AFFECTING OILSEED RAPE PROFITABILITY

Before Subsidy Change

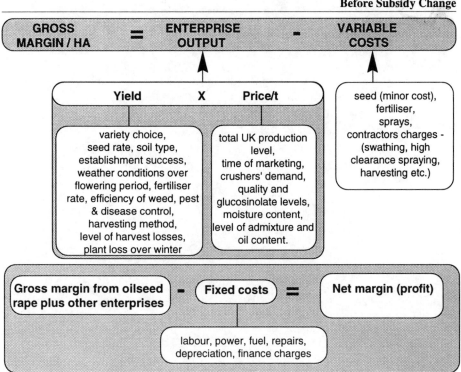

| GROSS MARGIN / HA | = | ENTERPRISE OUTPUT | - | VARIABLE COSTS |

Yield X **Price/t**

variety choice, seed rate, soil type, establishment success, weather conditions over flowering period, fertiliser rate, efficiency of weed, pest & disease control, harvesting method, level of harvest losses, plant loss over winter

total UK production level, time of marketing, crushers' demand, quality and glucosinolate levels, moisture content, level of admixture and oil content.

seed (minor cost), fertiliser, sprays, contractors charges - (swathing, high clearance spraying, harvesting etc.)

Gross margin from oilseed rape plus other enterprises - **Fixed costs** = **Net margin (profit)**

labour, power, fuel, repairs, depreciation, finance charges

1992 After Subsidy Change

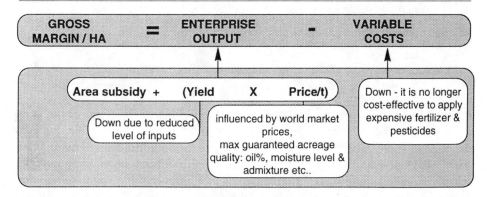

| GROSS MARGIN / HA | = | ENTERPRISE OUTPUT | - | VARIABLE COSTS |

Area subsidy + (**Yield** X **Price/t**)

Down due to reduced level of inputs

influenced by world market prices, max guaranteed acreage quality: oil%, moisture level & admixture etc..

Down - it is no longer cost-effective to apply expensive fertilizer & pesticides

PRODUCTION

MARKETING

MAIN PRODUCTS/OUTLETS

The UK produced approximately 1 million tonnes of oilseed rape in 1994. This was used as follows:

i   food manufacturing industry e.g. cooking oils, margarines etc.

ii soap and detergent industry

iii industrial uses e.g. paint manufacture and specialist lubricant

iv animal feed industry (compounding) utilises the protein rich residue after oil-extraction

---

QUALITY STANDARDS

Erucic acid content

An undesirable product in oilseed rape. Plant breeders have now reduced the erucic acid content of current UK varieties to below the 2% standard. A small market exists for high erucic acid rape oil for use as a specialist lubricant.

Glucosinolate content (measured in units of micro-moles)

These are the undesirable sulphur compounds inherently present in oilseed rape which limits the inclusion of oilseed rape meal in livestock rations.

Currently the maximum glucosinolate level stands at 35 micro-moles, and the EU has declared its intention to reduce this to 20 within two years. Few varieties presently available would guarantee to meet this standard. Samples failing to meet the standard would not attract EU financial support.

Hopefully in the near future, new and improved varieties will meet such standards.

Moisture content

Contracts usually based on a 9% moisture content basis. Higher moisture contents might be accepted but at a lower price.

Oil content

Usually based on 40% oil content. Higher and lower oil contents worth more or less according to the terms of the contract. High oil content varieties can be more profitable than higher yielding but lower oil content types.

Admixture (non oilseed rape seed)

Usually a maximum of 2% admixture is permitted, although allowances can be made. Admixture includes:

MARKETING

| volunteer cereal seeds | chaff | dirt and stones |
| weed seeds | pods | |

General Marketable Quality (G.M.Q.)

G.M.Q. refers to broken or damaged seed the maximum level allowed being 2%.

| no mouldy seeds | no live pests | no abnormal smells |

Agronomic Influences On Glucosinolate Content

i **Variety choice.** The single most important consideration. Variety glucosinolate levels likely to be further reduced through plant breeding.

ii **Volunteers.** These are from previous high glucosinolate rape crops and may increase overall glucosinolate levels slightly.

iii **Fungicide and insecticide treatments**. Crops protected against pests and diseases will tend to produce lower glucosinolate levels as well as producing other obvious yield benefits.

iv **Sulphur.** OSR is susceptible to sulphur deficiency, but over applications of sulphur can increase glucosinolate.

v **Timing of harvest.** Crops desiccated or swathed too early, contain a higher glucosinolate content.

Some Oilseed Rape Double Low Varieties

Winter	Features	Spring	Features
	Fully recommended		
Idol	Good yield, fairly responsive to fungicides.	Mars	High yielding
Samourai	Av yield. Very early to flower & ripen.	Starlight	High yielding
Falcon	Very late to flower.		
Envol	High yield, very responsive to fungicides. High oil content.		
	Provisional recommendation		
Bristol	Currently, the highest yielding variety on paper.		
Apex	Similar yield to Bristol but slower to ripen.		
Mandarin	Weak stem and prone to lodging.		
Express	Good resistance to lodging and stem canker.		
Apache	Very responsive to fungicides.		
Rocket	Good standing power.		

MARKETING

Note:

i   Provided quality standards are met, there is often no great distinction between varieties except with resistance to disease.

ii Winter oilseed rape crops when severely damaged by frost for example, are often replaced with spring sown oilseed rape.

iii Recommended OSR varieties are rapidly changing as newer higher yielding, lower glucosinolate, better disease resistant varieties are being introduced.

Winter Oilseed Rape - Variety Market Share

Variety	1991 %	1992 %	1994 %
Falcon	29	17	2
Envol	26	18	1
Libravo	12	6	1
Lictor	11	3	-
Capricorn	9	12	6
Samourai	4	1	-
Bristol	-	21	11
Rocket	2	2	1
Apache	-	14	4
Lineker	-	2	-
Others	-	4	6
Apex	-	-	63
Inca	-	-	4
Express	-	-	1

Source: ISP

OSR Seasonal Fluctuations In Price 1993/94

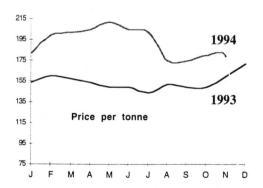

MARKETING

ENVIRONMENT

PREFERRED ENVIRONMENT

Climate

Oilseed rape prefers temperate climates. It is widely grown in Northern Europe and Canada (Canola). In more severe climatic areas e.g. in parts of Canada, Spring sown rape is grown. The climate throughout the UK is satisfactory although occasional harsh Winters can significantly reduce plant populations.

Adequate moisture during the critical Autumn establishment phase is important as is adequate pre-Winter growth. If there is not enough growth before the Winter, the crop may need resowing with a Spring variety. Dry, sunny conditions during flowering improve pollination contributing to yield.

Water Requirements

The 750 - 900 mm rainfall of the arable Eastern counties is usually adequate. Sufficient moisture during establishment is essential to ensure the crop emerges quickly and evenly before the onset of Winter.

Evaporation rates are still high during establishment in August and September and every effort must be made to conserve moisture during seedbed preparation.

Soil Type

Oilseed rape will grow satisfactorily on a wide range of soil types. The reduced water-holding capacity of light sandy soils can limit yields in drought season the highest yields being generally achieved on heavier moisture retentive soil-types provided compaction is not a problem.

Drainage

Oilseed rape is generally more susceptible to poor drainage than Winter cereals. In heavier (clay) soil conditions, pipe drainage is essential to ensure the Winter water table doesn't rise to within 0.5 m of the surface.

ROTATIONS

In much of England, oilseed rape is preceded by Winter barley, the early harvest of which enables timely establishment of the rape crop. Early maturing Winter wheat could be an alternative preceding crop. Set-aside has recently become an attractive entry for OSR because seedbed can be prepared well in advance.

In many areas of Scotland where even winter barley is harvested too late to establish successfully oilseed rape, Spring sown oilseed rape is preferred.

ENVIRONMENT

Following oilseed rape, Winter cereal is usually grown. Winter wheat benefits from:

- ☛ the break in cereal weed, pest and disease life cycles
- ☛ the remaining nitrogen
- ☛ the improved soil structure
- ☛ timely establishment

But

- ☛ beware slugs after oilseed rape.

Oilseed Typical Rotations

years	
1	Winter rape
2	Winter wheat
3	Winter wheat
4	Winter barley/Set-aside

Close cropping can encourage pest and disease build-up.

years	
1	Winter rape
2	Winter wheat
3	Peas/beans
4	Winter wheat
5	Set-aside

Peas/Spring beans and oilseed rape are all hosts for Sclerotinia disease, but Winter beans are affected by a different strain of the disease.

Note:

Avoid growing oilseed rape in adjacent fields in successive years, as this can encourage Phoma Stem Canker, transmitted from the previous crop stubble by wind blown spores.

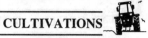

ENVIRONMENT

CULTIVATIONS

Seedbed Requirements

Fine	to ensure good seed to soil contact for rapid germination. Oilseed rape is a very small seed. Also improve the efficiency of soil-acting herbicides
Firm	to conserve early Autumn moisture
Free from	**compaction** which limits root development and therefore water and nutrient uptake reducing yields
Free from	**trash** which interferes with the drilling operations

Typical Cultivation Practices/Sequences

Direct drill	Reduced cultivation practice	Traditional approach
Sub-soil previous years' tramlines Direct drill [i]	Sub soil [ii] Disc x 2 Roll [iii]	Sub soil Plough ⌐ possibly Roll ⌐ combined plough & press
Roll/light harrow	Drill Light harrow Roll	Power harrow x 2 Roll Drill Light harrow Roll

Note:

i   direct drill without prior cultivations
ii only sub-soil if necessary to alleviate compaction
iii usually a Cambridge (ribbed) roller

	Estimated cost/ha	Estimated hours/ha
Direct drill	£25 - 35	1.5
Reduced cultivations	£60 - 80	3.0 - 3.5
Traditional approach	£80 - 100	4.0 - 5.0

Source: BASF Guide to
maximum Profits

ENVIRONMENT

CONTRACTOR COSTS

Task	Detail	Cost (£/ha)
Subsoiling	(450 mm deep, 1.2 m spacing)	54.11
Ploughing	over 230 mm deep	42.10
	+ press add	4.45
Disc harrow	(medium)	24.70
Power harrow		29.65
Rolling		14.85
Direct drilling into previous crop stubble		25.10
Power harrow and drill combination		45.95
Light harrow		19.75
Fertiliser application		8.90

Source: A.B.C.

Last Seasons Growing Environment (Harvest 1993)

Adequate moisture during the growing season allowed most crops to produce good yields. A showery harvest resulted inevitably in some crop losses. Late-maturing Spring rape crops were especially late to harvest with many crops harvested as late as October.

Current Season (Harvest 1994)

Ample moisture has allowed rape crops to get off to a good start. (Double-low varieties tend to be less vigorous and slower to establish). Crops'grown after set-aside have been badly affected by slug damage.

Effect Of N.S.A.'s (Nitrate Sensitive Areas)

Despite applying relatively large dressings of nitrogen (up to 200 kg/ha), relatively little is removed in the harvested crop. The remaining nitrogen, contained in stubble and trash etc., is returned to the soil where it may be leached in the following winter.

Consequently, growers of oilseed rape in N.S.A.'s have had their nitrogen applications restricted to a level 50 kg/ha lower than optimum.

THE OILSEED RAPE PRODUCTION CYCLE

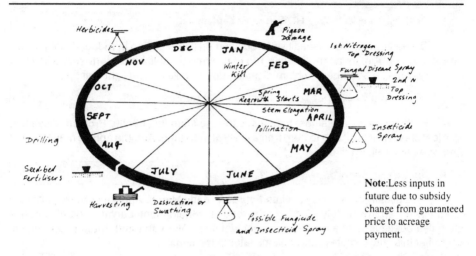

Note: Less inputs in future due to subsidy change from guaranteed price to acreage payment.

THE OILSEED RAPE GROWTH CYCLE

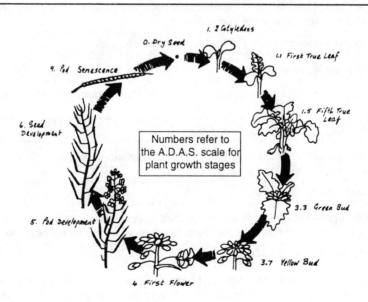

Numbers refer to the A.D.A.S. scale for plant growth stages

GROWTH STAGES

WINTER OILSEED RAPE

1 Drill last 2 weeks in August, first week September

Oilseed rape is very sensitive to delayed drilling resulting in reduced yield. **Seed rate** @ 7 kg/ha. Aim for approximately **100 plants/m²**. Establishment fertiliser 25 kg N/ha 50 kg P & K/ha on average. Problem disease, downy mildew and light leaf spot.

2 & 3 Apply herbicide treatments to control weeds

Problem pests are slugs, pigeons, cabbage stem flea beetle. Problem diseases, light leaf spot. Winter kill due to hard frosts likely at this stage. Autumn aphids may transmit Beet Western Yellows virus.

4 Spring re-growth

This usually commences in late February, early March. Apply first Spring nitrogen top-dressing, approximately $\frac{1}{3}$ to $\frac{1}{2}$ of the total N requirement. Larval stage of cabbage stem flea beetle a maybe a problem. Light leaf spot, Alternaria and Phoma may require control at this stage to prevent problems later in the season.

5 March/April.

Stem elongation and plant development particularly rapid at this stage. Apply the second N top dressing before the end of March.

6 Rapid stem growth often literally leaves diseases behind!

7 Pollen beetle and seed weevil

These may be present and pollen beetle needs to be controlled before the onset of full flower.

8 April/May

Cold wet conditions during this phase can seriously reduce pollen movement throughout the crop reducing yields significantly.

9 June

At 95% petal full, alternaria as well as seed weevil may require treatment to prevent pod damage. Earliest formed pods i.e. those lower down on the stem ripen first.

10 July - Pre harvest treatments

Because of the uneven maturity of pods, they must be forced to ripen evenly by a pre-harvest treatment either by killing the crop using a desiccant or swathing i.e. cutting the crop and laying it in swaths to be picked up later (dealt with in greater detail in 🧍).

NUTRIENT REQUIREMENTS

Oilseed rape is particularly sensitive to acidic conditions and a minimum soil pH of 6.0 is tolerable.

Winter oilseed rape	N, P or K Index		
Previous crop			
Soil type	0	1	2
Mineral	kg/ha nutrient		
Nitrogen (N)			
Seedbed	30	0	
Spring top dressing	2160	100	40
Peaty and organic			
Nitrogen (N) Seedbed	0	0	
Spring top dressing	100	50	0
All soils			
Phosphate (P_2O_5)	100	75M	50M
Potash (K_2O)	90	65M	40M
Spring oilseed rape			
Nitrogen (N)[ii]	120	60	0
Phosphate (P_2O_5)	100	75	50M
Potash (K_2O)	90	65	40M

Note:

i   Increase by 30kg/ha for each 0.5t/ha variation in yield from 3t/ha.

ii   On sandy soils and shallow soils over chalk or limestone, split the N application, apply half the top dressing at the start of the Spring growth & the remainder by early April. This is to prevent leaching.

Source: A.D.A.S. Fertiliser Recommendation Ref Book 209

NUTRITION

LEACHING OF NITROGEN

In response to growing environmental pressure growers are reducing Autumn nitrogen applications from 50 down to perhaps 30 kg/ha.

Oilseed rape commences growth in Spring earlier than other arable crops and should therefore be fertilised earlier, usually in late February. Heavy prolonged rainfall after early N applications can lead to leaching of soluble nitrates.

Following oilseed rape, the soil is assumed to have a nitrogen index of 1, therefore reduce nitrogen applications to the following cereal crop.

OTHER NUTRIENTS

Magnesium (Mg)

Oilseed rape crops very rarely respond to magnesium. On soils known to be deficient apply Kieserite (16% Mg) as required to suit rotational requirements.

Sulphur (S)

Although relatively large amounts may be required, (up to 70 kg/ha sulphur), this is usually supplied from soil reserves and atmospheric sulphur deposition. As atmospheric sulphur is reduced by environmental legislation we are likely to see sulphur deficiency in oilseed rape. In some areas, distant from industry, yield response to sulphur applications are often recorded. Unfortunately , an over supply of sulphur can increase undesirable glucosinolates.

Manganese (Mn)

This is rarely a problem. It is usually induced by over-application of lime which makes the manganese temporarily unavailable.

Boron (Bo)

Not usually a problem, except on light, sandy soils. Deficiencies can be corrected by a suitable trace-element spray.

NUTRIENT DEFICIENCY SYMPTOMS AND FACTORS

Nutrient	Predisposing Factors	Deficiency Symptoms
Nitrogen (N)	light soils and insufficient applied	limited leaf production small plants, light green in colour which results in early flowering and much reduced seed and oil yields
Phosphorus (P)	pH below 6.0.and poor root development due to compaction or water logging	dwarfed plants and leaves dark green to blue turning purple later, and older leaves die prematurely
Potassium (K)	soil pH below 5.5. Poor root development and/or failure to maintain adequate soil reserves	dwarf plants and reduced leaf area; leaves dark green with interveinal chlorosis (turning yellow due to lack of chlorophyll)
Magnesium (Mg)	poor root growth and soil naturally deficient in magnesium	chlorosis of older leaves becoming red and purple
Sulphur (S)	remote rural area, far removed from industrial sources of atmospheric sulphur; light soils	light green to yellow leaves; flower petals lighter coloured; poor pod fill
Boron	induced by high pH conditions, above 7.5; light soils are naturally lower in Boron	stunted growth, chlorotic rolled leaves; distortion of the flowers and poor seed set

TYPICAL OILSEED RAPE FERTILISERS

	N%	P%	K%	Approx. Cost £/t
Autumn compounds	17	17	17	120 - 135
	10	24	24	115 - 125
	0	24	24	98 - 105
	12	15	20	115 - 125
Spring top dressing	34.5			95 - 110
	46 (urea)			105 - 120

NUTRITION

TIMING OF FERTILISER APPLICATION

Winter Oilseed Rape

Provide all P and K and some N according to circumstances in the Autumn seedbed. For the Spring top dressing apply $\frac{1}{3}$ - $\frac{1}{2}$ of total nitrogen requirements towards the end of February, just before the start of Spring re-growth and rapid stem extension. Apply the remainder by late March.

Spring Oilseed Rape

All N, P and K in the seedbed unless there is a risk of leaching. If so, split the nitrogen as 50 kg/ha in the seedbed, the remainder by early May.

OILSEED RAPE GROWTH REGULATORS

Although the recently introduced double-low varieties are taller-strawed and therefore prone to lodging, considerable manipulation of the crop is possible without chemical growth regulators. For example, crops drilled at a lower seed rate, are shorter and with thicker stems and are far less likely to lodge. Chemical growth regulators have so far proved too variable in their effects to be useful, and too expensive.

WEEDS AND WEED CONTROL

Satisfactory Weed Control Is Essential To Ensure That:

i   the crop is able to achieve its full yield potential through the removal of weed competition

ii   the weed-free crop is far easier to harvest

iii   weed seeds adversely affect oil quality; for example charlock contains high levels of glucosinolates

iii   quality is maintained; weed seeds constitute **admixture**, and if greater than 2%, a lower price will be received

iv   in view of subsidy changes and the lack of sufficient yield response to cover herbicide costs, growers may not use them in future. However, competitive grass weeds and volunteers must still be controlled.

Main Problem Weeds

Grass weeds

Cereal volunteers, especially winter barley from the previous crop, can be very competitive.

Blackgrass Wild oats Barren brome Annual meadow grass	oilseed rape provides an ideal opportunity to control these problem grass weeds.
Couch (perennial)	better controlled in previous crops in the rotation.

Broadleaved weeds

Brassica weeds:	
Charlock Mustard Runch	almost impossible to control in rape which is also a brassica
Chickweed Mayweed Cleavers	competitive in the Autumn only expensive to control the seed is same size as oilseed rape and therefore is difficult to separate

HEALTH

Poppy	contaminates seed samples.
Polygonums:	
Knotgrass	only germinate in Spring therefore
Black bindweed	a problem in Spring rape crops.
Redshank	

WEED CONTROL STRATEGY

Light cultivations following harvest of the previous cereal crop will encourage any shed seeds to germinate and establish. Subsequent cultivations to estbalish the rape crop should control them effectively and cheaply.

Herbicide Selection

Must be safe to use on the crop and offer the best possible control of the current or expected weeds. It must also be cost effective.

Treatment types:

Pre-sowing	applied before the oilseed rape is drilled
Pre-emergence	applied after drilling but before the crop emerges
Post-emergence	herbicide must be selective i.e. kills the weeds but leaves the crop unaffected
Sequential programme	e.g. 2 herbicides applied in a sequence, 1 pre-emergence followed by a post-emergence
Residuals	most oilseed rape herbicides are residual in soils killing weeds as they establish. Some may be residual for several months

---

HEALTH

COMMON PESTS

Autumn/Winter	
Cabbage stem flea beetle	adult beetle damages the plant in Autumn, and its larvae cause damage in the Spring
Rape Winter stem weevil	still uncommon in the Northern region
Slugs	especially on heavier soils; and after set-aside rapeencourages slugs which are oftenparticularly damaging to following wheat crops
Pigeons	a serious pest, causing grazing damage which can be severe especially near wooded areas
Aphids	an increasing problem which trans-mits Beet Western Yellows Virus Disease
Spring/Summer	
Blossom/Pollen beetle	attracted by yellow flowers, but is not a serious problem and may actually encourage pollination more of a problem in spring rape.
Cabbage seed weevil	larvae feed on developing seeds within the pod and treatment is often justified
Brassica pod midge	very small fly whose eggs laid within the pod hatch into larvae which eat the pod lining leading to serious seed loss

---

Pest Control Strategy

The grower should keep in mind various methods to control crop pests. For example, pigeons may be controlled through organised shooting, or using bangers, kites etc.; slugs using slug pellets applied during crop establishment.

HEALTH

It should be noted that very few insecticide products are approved for use during the flowering phase. Most products can be applied before or after flowering to prevent killing beneficial bees.

COMMON DISEASES AND THEIR SIGNIFICANCE

Light leaf spot	relatively common (high levels in 1994)
Downy mildew	this can be serious at the cotyledon (emergence) stage of growth but rarely a problem
Botrytis	also known as Grey Mould and is associated with warm damp conditions when it attacks damaged plants
Sclerotinia	increasing in significance as the area of susceptible crops e.g. oilseed rape, peas and spring beans has increased
Alternaria	can be a serious disease on the pods and causes premature ripening.
Stem canker (phoma)	many double-low varieties are more susceptible to this disease. Leaf symptoms often seen in the Autumn.

Disease Control Strategy

It is essential that growers destroy or prevent volunteer oilseed rape plants which harbour disease. Whenever possible use resistant varieties and avoid growing oilseed rape more frequently than **one year in five**, even though this may not be the most profitable option. In addition, use the appropriate fungicidal seed treatments and sprays.

TYPICAL OILSEED RAPE SPRAYS AND COSTS

Spray	£/ha
Herbicide	35 - 55
Insecticide	5 - 20
Fungicide	16 - 25
Desiccant	20 - 38

SPRAY EQUIPMENT COSTS

Item	Detail	Cost £
12 m wide mounted sprayer	600 - 800 litre	2,000 - 10,000
24 m trailed sprayer	2,500 litre	20,000

Source: A.B.C.

LEGAL ASPECTS

F.E.P.A. (Food And Environmental Protection Act)

Covers the application of all pesticides. Intended to safeguard the operator, the eventual consumer and the environment as a whole.

C.O.S.H.H.

Control of Substances Hazardous to Health. A further development of the Health and Safety at Work Act. It is the responsibility of the employer to make an adequate assessment of the risks from hazardous materials, (including pesticides, micro-organisms, dust etc.) and decide on the control measures to prevent exposure.

HEALTH

AIMS

Oilseed rape harvest losses average about 120kg/ha (£18.00/ha assuming rape is worth £150/tonne). The aim is to minimise these losses and in doing this the following should be taken into account:

i   oilseed rape matures rapidly starting from the earliest formed pods, those lower down on the stem. Rape flowers for approximately 1 month and throughout this period, pods are continually being formed. A considerable range of pod maturity can therefore exist on the same plant

ii   pre-harvest treatment is necessary to ensure all pods ripen at roughly the same time

iii   early formed pods may shatter and shed their seed unless harvesting is accurately timed

iv   for prolonged, safe storage, moisture content should be reduced to 8%. The drier the oilseed rape at the point of harvest, the lower will be any drying costs.

PRE-HARVEST TREATMENTS

Desiccation

One method is to apply a desiccant which literally dries out the crop and therefore kills it, forcing the pods to ripen evenly. This is the ideal method when the crop is badly lodged.

Advantages	Disadvantages
no specialist equipment required although a wide boom sprayer would minimise crop damage	possible shatter of pods under windy conditions
crop dries quicker after rain	need to travel through tall crop just before harvest
less weather dependent	contractor often required for
cleaner seed samples	wide boom spraying e.g. 24 metres
good weed control	

HARVESTING

Swathing

Swathing involves cutting the crop, usually with a self-propelled swather and leaving the crop on the stubble to dry out helped by air passing beneath the swath. However, this is not a suitable technique for lodged crops.

Advantages	Disadvantages
less pod-shatter in windy conditions	dependent upon availability of contractor
no running in the crop before harvest	more weather susceptible
greater harvester work rates	crop takes longer to dry after rain
	risk of seed sprouting within the swath

Direct Combining

Direct combining without any pre-harvest treatment is particularly suitable to Spring oilseed rape, though this technique has been successfully uised in winter oilseed rape. This is because the Spring crop flowers over a shorter time period so the pods mature evenly.

OILSEED RAPE - HARVEST MANAGEMENT

Method	Seed colour in pods from main stem		
	Bottom pods	Middle third	Top pods
Desiccation	dark brown to black	reddish brown to dark brown	green to brown
Swathing	dark brown	reddish brown	green
Direct combine	black	black	dark brown

Oilseed Quality Criteria

Desiccating or swathing too early can increase glucosinolate content. Harvest the crop when it is as near 8% moisture content as possible provided this doesn't increase field losses. Minimise any admixture e.g. weed seeds, chaff, seed pods, soil and stones.

HARVESTING

Post-Harvest Care

Note:

Oilseed Rape is small seeded and will easily escape through small holes in combines, trailers, crop stores etc. It should be dried slowly but immediately after harvest down to 8% moisture content and stored at 10°C. The maximum drying depth for on-floor bulk drying systems is 1.2 metres. Once dried, the crop can be stored much deeper.

Straw (Crop Residue) Disposal

Straw is usually chopped, either on the combine or as a separate operation to make it easier to incorporate. Lightly cultivate to encourage any shed seed to germinate and then destroy them by spraying or subsequent cultivation.

Since 1992 burning of straw is banned necessitating incorporation.

HARVESTING EQUIPMENT AND COSTS

The cost of a self propelled combine, varies according to size from £30,000 to £115,000. Considerably cheaper second hand machines can be purchased. Leasing and more recently, short term hire schemes are increasing in popularity.

Storage

A bulk grain drying and storage building (on the floor drying system), cost approximately £120 for every tonne of capacity e.g. 500 tonne store, will cost £60,000. It is possible to have your crop contract stored - i.e. a contractor stores your crop until you decide to sell, for approximately 30p/tonne/week.

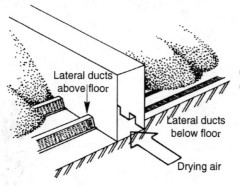

Diagram shows details of a floor drying system and the flow of air into air ducts under the crop.

HARVESTING

CONTRACTORS CHARGES

Operation	Cost (£/ha)
Swathing	32.10
Combining	88.95
High clearance sprayer for desiccation (excluding chemical costs)	10.65
Drying oilseed rape down to 8% moisture	£/t
from 20% moisture	16.75
from 16% moisture	14.25

Source: A.B.C.

TYPICAL GROSS MARGIN

	Winter £/ha	Spring £/ha
Output/ha		
Yield 3.t at £150/t	450	
Yield 2.t at £150/t		315
* Subsidy est. 1995	405	405
Output	**855**	**720**
Variable costs/ha		
Seed	40	
Seed		42.5
Fertiliser	75	
Fertiliser		50
Chemicals	85	52.5
TOTAL	**278**	**202**

Source: J. Nix 1994

* Depending on the value of the green pound, world price and UK Base Area.

Note:

i   The switch from single to double low varieties (low in both erucic acid and glucosinolates) is now virtually complete. EU price support for single lows was withdrawn after 1991.

ii   Samples failing to meet the current 35 micro-mole glucosinolate standard and in future the 20 micro-mole standard will not be eligible for EU support.

FIXED COSTS

Profitable farms manage to **minimise fixed costs**, and to **maximise output** from their type of farming system so that fixed costs per unit output are as low as possible.

PERFORMANCE

The figures below are typical levels of fixed costs for arable farms. Individual farms will vary in their levels of fixed costs for specific reasons - e.g. new farms will have high **rental charges of 40% to 70%** higher than those quoted. **Larger farms** will tend to have lower costs/hectare.

Farm type	TOTAL FIXED COSTS (£/ha)		
	<100 ha	100 - 200 ha	>200 ha
Intensive Arable	918	750	641
	<100 ha	100 - 200 ha	>200 ha
Mixed cropping, more than 50% gross output from cash cropping.	702	670*	568

Source: A.B.C.

Fixed Cost Elements

*The table below shows the components of these fixed costs:

Item - Mixed Cropping Farm (100-200ha)	£/ha
Regular labour	220
Depreciation	125
Repairs, tax and insurance - equipment	60
Fuel and electricity	45
Contract charges - hedging/ditching	15
Land maintenance (fencing, repairs etc.)	20
Rent & rates	135
Fees, office expenses	50
TOTAL	**670**

Source: A.B.C.

OUTSIDER'S GUIDE

Average Tenant's Capital

This is the value of investment normally provided by the tenant for items such as machinery, crops in store and other assets required to run the business.

Mixed Cropping Farm of over 100 ha	£/ha
Livestock	275
Crops and cultivations	370
Machinery & equipment	475
TOTAL	**1120**

Source: A.B.C.

Sensitivity

The table below shows how the gross margin varies with changes in the price of Winter oilseed rape and the yield per hectare. It is assumed that variable costs are £278 per hectare, and the area payment is £459/ha.

Yield t/hectare	1.4	1.6	1.8	2.0	2.2	2.4	2.6	2.8
Price £ per tonne	Gross margins £ per hectare							
140	492	520	548	576	604	632	660	688
145	504	533	562	591	620	649	678	707
150	516	546	576	606	636	666	696	726
155	528	559	590	621	652	683	714	745
160	540	572	604	636	668	700	732	764
165	552	585	618	651	684	717	750	783
170	564	598	632	666	700	734	768	802
175	576	611	646	681	716	751	786	821
180	588	624	660	696	732	768	804	840

Source: ABC

OUTSIDER'S GUIDE

THE
OUTSIDER'S GUIDE
to
PEAS & BEANS

1995 Edition

TOTAL PRODUCTION (WORLD GROWERS)

Peas, beans and other legume crops have been grown as a protein source to supplement cereals since prehistoric times. Russia and China between them grow about 70% of the world's peas and beans, approximately 14 million tons.

Peas are grown for fresh consumption, and to be harvested dry by conventional combine harvesters. Beans (species *Vicia faba*) are grown to be harvested dry, and are mainly used for livestock feed.

PRODUCTION IN THE EU

Since the introduction of the European Community Scheme to encourage the production of home grown protein for livestock feed, the area of peas and beans grown in the EU has grown to 939,000 ha and 360,000 ha respectively. France is the major pea grower with 680,000 ha whilst the UK accounts for the largest field bean area at 148,000 ha.

Production Trends And Cycles

Peas are a notoriously risky crop to grow, being highly susceptible to wet conditions, especially during flowering and harvest time. Consequently the area of peas grown depends on the previous year's weather, with plantings usually well down after a wet year, e.g. 1987.

In the UK only 40% of feed compounders demand for protein is being met by peas, so a further increase in production seems likely. Beans are presently being overproduced for the home market, but export opportunities do exist.

The recent introduction of white-flowered, low tannin bean varieties, more suitable for inclusion in livestock rations, should stimulate futher demand for the crop

Like nearly all arable crops, profitability largely depends on EU price support. Increasing financial pressure could reduce the level of support in the near future.

UK Pea And Bean Production Trends

In 1994 field bean area was down about 9% on the previous year of 163,100 hectares. Dried peas were down by about 1% at 80,200 hectares.

45,100ha of peas produced annually are for the vining and fresh pea market. The area of vining peas has declined by 10% on the previous 50,490ha. A limited amount of vining peas are exported. Some peas are imported from other EU countries e.g. France where the crop is subsidised.

PRODUCTION

The dried pea hectareage has declined since the high point in 1987 largely as a result of disappointing yields and a reduction in the minimum guaranteed price. Meanwhile, the field bean hectareage is levelling out after peaking in 1988 nd again in 1993. It is interesting to note that the field bean hectareage has always exceeded that of dry harvested peas since 1987.

The hectareage of both crops could increase in future, due to improved varieties with higher and consistent yields and the encouraging EU hectareage payment, currently 385ECU/ha.

Why Grow Peas And Beans?

Break crops are used to rest soil from cereal production, which is the main stay of most arable farms. Peas and beans make ideal break crops, as they:

- reduce weed, pest and disease problems in future cereal crops

Counties Growing
Vining Peas

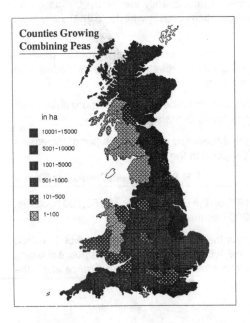

Counties Growing
Combining Peas

in ha

- 10001–15000
- 5001–10000
- 1001–5000
- 501–1000
- 101–500
- 1–100

- improve soil structure and provide nitrogen to the soil
- increase the yield and profitability of following cereal crops
- require no specialist equipment (except vining peas)
- produce a profit similar to cereals
- spread labour and machinery workload more evenly throughout the year
- tie up less capital than autumn sown crops
- reduce the risk of crop failure or market collapse compared to an all cereal farm.

OUTSIDER'S GUIDE

	Peas			Beans		
	'91	'92	'93	'91	'92	'93
Area ('000ha)	69	79	80.2	131	129	163.1
Yield (t/ha)	3.56	3.55	3.50	3.28	3.78	3.50
Production ('000t)	244	265	281	429	487	571

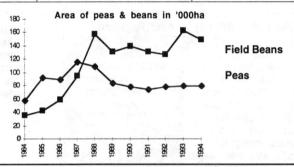

Area of peas & beans in '000ha

Field Beans

Peas

KEY ASSESSMENT QUESTIONS

	Vining Peas	Protein Peas	Field Beans Winter	Field Beans Spring
Yields (t/ha)	4.8	3.7	4.0	3.7
Output (£/ha)	984	744	735	718
Total Variable Costs (£/ha)	584	216	172	166
Gross margin (£/ha)	400	529	546	569

Source: A.B.C.

FACTORS AFFECTING PROFITABILITY

Ultimately profitability depends on the EU acreage payment (currently 385.45ECU/ha) and world market prices. Individual farmers can do nothing to change this, but can adjust acreages grown as a result of studying EU policy statements and production trends.

Individual farmers can optimise the profitability of their crops by following husbandry and marketing guidelines as laid out later in this guide. A general "rule of thumb" is that each input should be carefully scrutinised in terms of extra output obtained from its use.

PRODUCTION

FACTORS AFFECTING PROFITABILITY

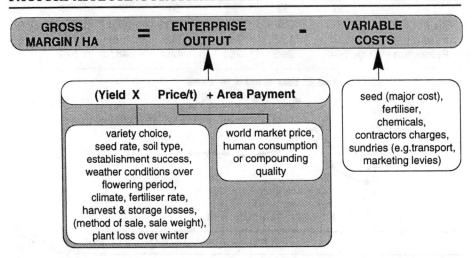

| GROSS MARGIN / HA | = | ENTERPRISE OUTPUT | − | VARIABLE COSTS |

(Yield X Price/t) + Area Payment

variety choice, seed rate, soil type, establishment success, weather conditions over flowering period, climate, fertiliser rate, harvest & storage losses, (method of sale, sale weight), plant loss over winter

world market price, human consumption or compounding quality

seed (major cost), fertiliser, chemicals, contractors charges, sundries (e.g.transport, marketing levies)

Gross margin from peas & beans plus other enterprises − **Fixed costs** = **Net margin (Profit)**

labour, power, fuel, repairs, depreciation, finance charges

MARKETING

MAIN PRODUCTS

Crop	Primary product	Secondary product
Vining peas	Frozen and canned peas	Pea haulm: aid to soil fertility/structure when incorporated
Fresh peas	Peas sold in the pod	Pea haulm
Dried peas for human consumption	Canning, packets and split peas	Straw may be used for livestock feed
Dried peas	Livestock feed Micronised for pet food	Straw may be used for livestock feed
Beans	Livestock feed seed pigeons	Straw can be used to fuel straw burning central heating boilers or incorporated into the soil to aid structure and fertility

The major use of peas and beans is as a protein source in livestock rations. Peas are the better source, as beans contain tannin in their seed coat, which inhibits digestibility. Consequently, **peas fetch on average £11/tonne more than beans.**

Plant breeders have recently produced beans with much lower tannin levels (white seeded beans), which could greatly increase the demand, for UK beans.

UK MARKET OUTLETS AND UK CONSUMPTION

Peas

Peas & Beans minimum prices 93/94

Vining peas have the highest output, and the highest cost, due to the need for specialist harvesting equipment (pea viners) and rapid transport to factories prior to freezing.

Minimal quantities of peas are imported. Pea exports are rarely significant, occurring only when EU currency fluctuations allow trade to be profitable.

MARKETING

Peas

Market	Annual demand (tonnes)	Value/tonne (1992/93)	Ave. yield /hectare *	Average output per hectare (£) (excl. ha paym't)
Livestock feed	250,000	105	4.1	430
Seed	21,000	126	3.3	416
Canning	23,000	140	3.0	420
Vining	200,000	200	4.8	960
Split peas	3000	115	3.3	380
Pet food	10,000	115	3.3	380
Export	9000	135	3.0	405

*Yields are 10 year pea averages (Source: P.G.R.O.)

Beans

Minimal quantities of beans are imported. Like peas, bean exports are favoured by EU currency fluctuations allowing profitable trade.

Winter bean yields are on average 5% higher than spring beans. Costs however, are correspondingly higher resulting in similar levels of profitability.

Market	Annual demand (tonnes)	Value/tonne (1993/94)	Ave. yield /hectare *	Average output /hectare (£) (Excl. ha paym't)
Livestock feed	500,000	98	3.13	306
Seed	20,000	118	3.13	369
Canning for export	1000	118	3.13	369
Export for feed	20,000	98	3.13	306
Pigeons	10,000	120	3.13	375

*Yields are 10 year bean averages (Source: PGRO)

MARKETING

VARIETIES AND MARKETS

Vining (Fresh) Peas

These are invariably grown under contract, and variety choice is not the farmer's decision. A constant stream of crops reaching the correct stage of maturity must be achieved in each area, to allow pea vining machines to harvest each crop in turn. Yield suffers if crops are harvested too early, quality suffers if harvest is delayed.

Vining Pea Quality Standards

Colour   must be bright, attractive and a uniform green.

Flavour   crucial with additive free frozen peas.

Size   different grades are used for different products. Small seeded "Petit Pois" fetch a considerable premium, but are low yielding.

Skin Toughness   Harvesting delay and adverse growing conditions result in tough skinned peas which retail at a considerable discount. The "Tenderometer Test" is used by processors to measure this trait, and the resulting reading greatly affects price.

Dried Peas

Market	Preferred variety	Others accepted
Canning marrowfats	Maro, Bunting	Progreta, Guido
Packet marrowfats	Maro, Bunting	Progreta, Princess
Export marrowfats	Maro	Progreta
Canning small blues	Conquest	Orb
Packet large blues	Solara	Arena
Split peas	Bohatyr	Rex
Animal feed compounding	any	including processing rejects.

Quality standards for human consumption

Correct colour, flavour and texture The percentage of waste and stain in the sample must be low. Mn deficiency (causes Marsh Spot) an internal discolouration. Moisture content should be 16% or less according to contract. Samples must be free from taint, damage and pests.

Quality standards for livestock consumption (feed and compounding)

Maximum 14% moisture content with less than 3% impurities, and protein content should be approximately 24%.

MARKETING

All varieties are fully or provisionally recommended by the National Institute of Agricultural Botany (NIAB).

Varieties grown for premium human consumption markets tend to be lower yielding and costlier to grow than feed varieties. Price premiums offset this in most years. Export potential exists with all varieties, particularly with Maro.

As a general rule for all beans, above **18% moisture or 5% admixture** the buyer has the right to reject the delivery.

Field Beans Varieties And Quality Standards

	Variety	Market	Quality standards
WINTER	Bourdon Punch Boxer Glacier Striker	Livestock feed compounding	maximum 14% moisture and 3% admixture
SPRING	Maris Bead	Pigeon feed	small even size; required colour; no admixture & taint small size essential
	Alfred Mars	Export Livestock feed	Flat large pale seeded varieties required
	Victor Gobo Brok Erfano	Livestock feed compounding	maximum 14% moisture and less than 3% admixture.
	Vasco(W) Caspar (W) Cresta (W) Nevo(W)	Livestock feed	White flowered, tannin free varieties

Note: Any price premiums for white-flowered tannin free types is likely to decline in future as their production expands. Perhaps one day all beans will be white flowered with seed coats.

All above varieties are either provisionally or fully recommended by NIAB.

MARKETING

THE REVISED ARABLE SUPPORT SYSTEM FOR PEAS & BEANS

Since 1st July 1993:-

Prices Reduced

The minimum price and compounding subsidy arrangements for protein crop (i.e. peas and beans) has been discontinued.

Compensatory Payments

To compensate for the loss in income, hectareage payments have been introduced. These vary according to the area of a particular crop grown and will also vary on a regional basis according to historic yields.

Set Aside

Receipt of compensatory payments will depend upon meeting certain set-aside requirements, normally 15% or 18%, (this will be reduced in 1995 only) of the combinable crop acreage for all but very small farmers.

Stabiliser Withdrawn

The current arrangements to discourage over-production of particular crops by way of a Maximum Guaranteed Quantity (M.G.Q), above which, the minimum price is reduced, has been withdrawn.

Vining Peas

Producing seed for vining peas and the fresh pea market does qualify for area aid payments.

Eligibility

Claims for area payments can only be made on land used to grow the following crops:

1   Cereals, including wheat, durum wheat, barley, oats, rye, triticale, linseed.

2   Oilseeds, in the UK oilseed rape and a tiny acreage of sunflowers.

3   Dried peas and beans for harvest, sweet lupins and linseed.

MARKETING

Pulses

Regional cereal yields determine the protein crop hectareage ie. 2.6 x cereal payment.

Regional Payment Rates 1993 - 95

Crop	Regional Hectareage Payments			
	England	Scotland	Wales	N.Ireland
Cereals 1994	203.55	181.78	168.73	153.71
*Cereals 1995	193.53	233.72	216.94	197.63
Protein crops '94	248.83	337.59	313.35	285.47
Set-aside	359.41	296.04	274.78	250.34
LFA - Less Favoured Area				

*Will vary depending on value of ECU. Fixed by the UK green rate in force on 1 July of marketing year.

Payment

Payment for protein crops will normally be made between 16th October and 31st December of the harvest year.

Sowing

All crops must be sown by the 15th May.

Deadlines

Producers must apply for the area payments by the 15th May.

ENVIRONMENT

CLIMATE

The drier climate of the east of England is preferred. Southern France provides the ideal climate for these crops. Rain showers during flowering does increase yields, though too much rain during flowering leads to fungal disease (botrytis), and too much rainfall after flowering will reduce yield and quality (especially peas).

SOILS

Very light soils hold insufficient moisture, otherwise soil tolerances are as shown in the following table:

Soil type	Peas	S.beans	W.beans	Remarks
Sandy	✓			irrigation helpful
Loamy	✓	✓	✓	
Clayey		✓	✓	difficult to get spring seedbed
Organic	✓	✓		beware manganese deficiency and lodging

In addition, legumes are very susceptible to **soil compaction.**

DRAINAGE

Good drainage is essential, excess water can:

> **stunt root growth and nitrogen fixation**
> **make crops more drought susceptible**
> **increase foot rots (fusarium sp)**
> **hinder seedbed cultivations and crop establishment**
> **increase soil compaction hazard**
> **all of which will result in lower yields and quality.**

ENVIRONMENT

ROTATIONS

Minimum frequency is1 year in 5 i.e. 4 years without peas, beans or oilseed rape to avoid a risk of pea cyst nematode, downy mildew, pea wilt. Oilseed rape may carry over sclerotinia, an increasing problem in arable rotations.

There are a number of advantages arising from the growth of peas and beans in a rotation:

i Peas and beans are a good pest and disease break for cereals. Beans enable the use of powerful grass weed herbicides and can therefore be considered as cleaning crops in cereal rotations.

ii Peas and beans are leguminous and thus leave valuable reserves of nitrogen.

iii Peas provide a good entry for winter wheat but beware wheat bulb fly following vining crops. Beans will provide a good entry unless they are late maturing, in which case winter wheat drilling may be delayed.

Warning

It may be necessary to plough after the pea crop if certain soil residual herbicides have been used. Root crops provide a poor entry because of the risks of compacted soil and volunteers. The vast majority of pea and bean crops are grown as break crops following a cereal.

Example rotations:

Heavy land

Beans
Winter wheat
Winter wheat
Set-aside
Oilseed rape
Winter wheat
Winter Wheat

Light land

Peas
Winter barley
Winter barley
Sugar beet or potatoes
Set-aside

ENVIRONMENT

CULTIVATIONS

Crop / Cultivation	Peas & Spring Beans	Winter Beans
Primary cultivation	plough early	plough seed in
Secondary cultivation	harrow or power harrow avoid compaction conserve moisture	harrow in early spring for: weed control soil aeration plant number adjustment
Ideal seedbed	fine (with small aggregates to prevent capping of soil surface) roll to depress stones and conserve moisture after drilling	coarse so as to: protect plants through winter improve surface drainage (spray herbicide after any secondary cultivation)

ESTABLISHMENT

Plant Population

Optimum plant population (having accounted for seed costs):

Plant type	Plants/m²
Vining peas	90
Marrowfats	65
Large blue and large seeded whites	70
Small blues and small seeded whites	95
Leafless whites	100
Winter beans (post winter)	12 - 20
Spring beans	40 - 60

Source: P.G.R.O.

ENVIRONMENT

Factors affecting plant population

The achievement of the desired plant population above is affected by a number of factors. These include: seed size, seedbed losses which may amount to between 5 and 20% (depending upon sowing conditions for spring crops and the severity of the winter weather for winter crops), germination capacity of the seed used (minimum should be 85%) which reflects seed vigour and health.

Sowing Date

Crop	Optimum sowing time
Winter beans	November
Spring beans	February/March
Dried peas	March
Vining peas and beans	February to May (dictated by contract & continuity of production)

Early sowing of winter beans can lead to excessive winter kill. But early sowing of spring crops can lead to a number of benefits such as:

higher yields

superior quality

earlier maturity

However, only sow if conditions are suitable i.e. dry enough to avoid compaction.

Sowing

Winter bean seed is usually ploughed down in order to keep seed out of reach of rooks as well as to provide frost protection for seedlings and to improve surface drainage.

Spring beans and peas are usually sown with a conventional drill to a depth of 1.5 - 2.0 inches (35 - 50 mm). Drilling too fast can lead to uneven emergence and should be avoided.

Seed Treatment

Some seed treatments just prevent pre-emergence seed rots, while others give additional control of deep-seated seed borne infections.

ENVIRONMENT

VARIETAL CHOICE

Refer to National Institute of Agricultural Botany lists for latest varieties.

First consideration is the end **market** (related to pea type) such as feed, seed or human consumption; the second is the **yield,** and the third various agronomic characteristics shown in the table below.

Agronomic characteristic	Significance
Standing ability	choose strong standing varieties on fertile sites to prevent lodging & harvest difficulties
Shortness of straw	related to standing ability
Ease of combining	important with peas; related to standing ability
Maturity	important not to choose late maturing varieties in the north
Disease resistance	varying importance depending on disease; may be able to reduce fungicide costs

Vining pea and bean varieties are usually dictated by the processor.

LEGAL ASPECTS

Spring drilled crops like peas and spring beans are not ideal for Nitrogen Sensitive Areas (N.S.A.'s) because there is no crop cover through the winter which would otherwise utilise the nitrogen reserves.

However, legumes are beneficial in that they do not require applications of artificial nitrogen which might leach into water courses.

ENVIRONMENT

CULTIVATION EQUIPMENT AND COSTS

Item	Detail	Cost (£)
Ploughs:		
Mounted	4 - 5 furrow	2500 - 4800
Reversible	4 - 5 furrow	500 - 15000
Furrow Press /packer	**1.1 - 11 m**	**2000 - 11000**
Subsoiler	1 - 6 tine	700 - 7500
Spring tine cultivator	**2.5 - 4.3 m**	**1000 - 4500**
Disc harrows heavy, trailed	2.7 - 4.7m	5000 - 11,450
Power harrow	1.3 - 4.0 m	3500 - 12500
Rolls: triple gang	**4.2 - 12.8 m**	**4000 - 14000**
Seed drill:		
mounted	2.4 - 6.0 m	3000 - 15500
trailed	3.0 - 6.0 m	6500 - 17500
pneumatic	2.5 - 4.0 m	3000 - 10000

Source: A.B.C.

CONTRACTORS CHARGES

Operation	£/ha
Ploughing	30.20
Subsoiling	54.11
Spring tine harrowing	18.55
Medium disc harrowing	27.20
Power harrowing	29.65
Rolling	14.85
Drilling (1 man, seed in field)	19.75

Source: A.B.C.

THE WINTER BEAN PRODUCTION CYCLE

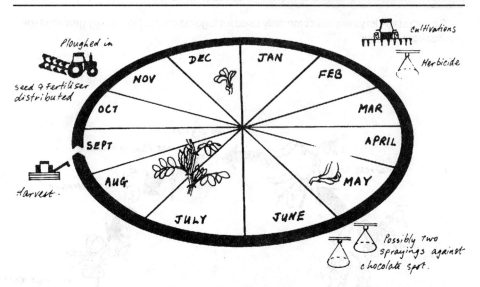

Ploughed in

Seed & Fertiliser distributed

Harvest.

Cultivations

Herbicide

Possibly two sprayings against chocolate spot.

(cycle wheel labelled: JAN, FEB, MAR, APRIL, MAY, JUNE, JULY, AUG, SEPT, OCT, NOV, DEC)

THE SPRING BEANS AND DRIED PEA PRODUCTION CYCLE

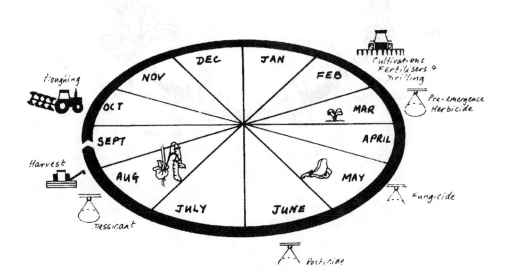

Ploughing

Harvest

Dessicant

Cultivations Fertilisers & Drilling

Pre-emergence Herbicide

Fungicide

Pesticide

(cycle wheel labelled: JAN, FEB, MAR, APRIL, MAY, JUNE, JULY, AUG, SEPT, OCT, NOV, DEC)

GROWTH STAGES

A LEGUME GROWTH CYCLE - PEAS

Growth stage keys are not commonly used for legume crops. Typical key growth stages are illustrated below.

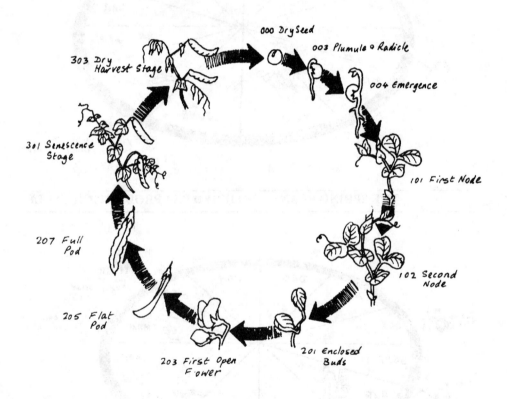

000 Dry Seed

003 Plumule ∘ Radicle

004 Emergence

101 First Node

102 Second Node

201 Enclosed Buds

203 First Open Flower

205 Flat Pod

207 Full Pod

301 Senescence Stage

303 Dry Harvest Stage

DRIED PEAS KEY GROWTH STAGES FOR FARM OPERATIONS

Growth stage	Action where necessary
Emergence	Use pre-emergence herbicides before this stage
Enclosed bud	Use MCPB herbicides before this stage Use pea midge insecticide
Visible bud	Begin aphicide spray programme, provided the threshold is met
Pod set	Use pea moth insecticide Use manganese spray Use Botrytis fungicide

Earliest Suitable Stage For Desiccation Of Dried Peas

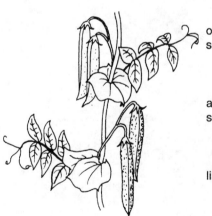

Top pods are fleshy, slightly pitted and green or starting to turn yellow and the seed splits if squeezed.

Middle pods are pitted and crinkled, yellow and becoming parchment-like in texture. and the seed is rubbery.

Bottom pods are yellow/brown, parchment-like (paper thin) and the seeds are quite hard.

Source: ICI Plant Protection

Crop desiccation with for example "Reglone" or "Challenge" is useful where crops are ripening unevenly or where weeds have been poorly controlled.

GROWTH STAGES

NUTRIENT REQUIREMENTS

Nitrogen, Phosphate & Potash

Peas and beans are legumes which means that they benefit from a symbiotic relationship with Rhizobium bacteria. These bacteria are present in the root nodules of leguminous crops and can supply the plant with nitrogen fixed from the air. No artificial nitrogen is therefore required for most legume crops.

Peas and beans	N, P, K or Mg Index		
Previous crop			
	0	**1** kg/ha	**2**
Broad beans for marketing and processing			
Nitrogen (N)	60	25	nil
Phosphate (P_2O_5)	250	200	150
Potash (k_2O)	250	150	100
French beans			
Nitrogen(N)	150	100	75
Phosphate (P_2O_5)	250	200	150
Potash (K_2O)	275	175	100
Field beans			
Phosphate (P_2O_5)	75	50	30M
Potash (K_2O)	120	50	30M
Peas for fresh market vining or combine			
Nitrogen (N)	nil	nil	nil
Phosphate (P_2O_5)	75	50	25
Potash (K_2O)	120	50	25
Beans and peas			
Magnesium (Mg)	150	100	nil

Source: M.A.F.F. Reference Book 209

NUTRITION

☛ For broad, french and runner beans, reduce the nitrogen by 90 kg/ha if Rhizobium inoculation is used.

☛ Nitrogen 25 kg.ha N should be broadcast for the early fresh pea market crop when spring rainfall has been unusually high.

☛ There is a risk to germination of peas if more than 50 kg/ha K_2O is combine drilled.

Lime

Peas and beans will not tolerate acidic conditions and thus the pH should be maintained above 6.5. However, overliming will cause lock-up of micro nutrients, particularly Manganese (Mn), possible leading to marsh spot (Mn deficiency) in peas.

Micro Nutrients

Manganese deficiency is the most common micro nutrient deficiency causing the Marsh Spot symptom in peas, where the centre of the pea becomes brown and unsuitable for human consumption or the seed markets.

Manganese sprays are available and must be apllied with a wetter to increase uptake through the foliage.

NUTRIENT APPLICATION

 ### Timing Of Application

Macro nutrients (e.g. P, K and Mg) should be applied to the seedbed before sowing or through the seed drill, or even down last year's tramlines.

Micro nutrients (e.g. Mn) should be sprayed at the first sign of deficiency (leaf yellowing in the case of manganese).

More than one application may be necessary.

NUTRITION

Methods Of Application

Combine drilling	Fertiliser and seed are delivered through the same drill coulter. There is a risk of the seed being scorched with higher rates of fertiliser. Fertiliser placed within easy reach of developing roots. Rarely practised today.
Broadcasting	Fertiliser is broadcast before the drilling of seed. This avoids seed scorch, but the fertiliser is not within easy reach of developing roots and thus higher application rates are necessary where P and K are deficient. This is the most common method.

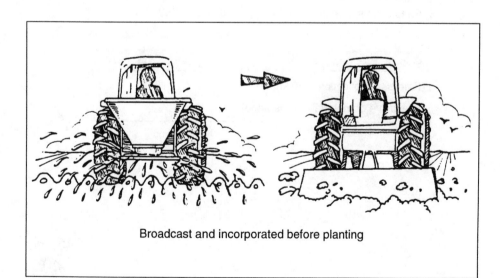

Broadcast and incorporated before planting

NUTRITION

Inoculation

The inoculation of seed with Rhizobium bacteria may be of benefit where new crops are introduced to a particular site, e.g. in the case of french beans.

GROWTH REGULATORS

There are currently no plant growth regulators approved for use in peas and beans although developmental work is in progress. Plant breeders have already been particularly successful in reducing height in the pea crop and improving harvesting.

FERTILISING EQUIPMENT AND COSTS

Equipment	£
Mounted spinner (210 - 2500 litre hopper)	600 - 5500
Trailed spinner (1250 - 5000 litre hopper)	2750 - 10500
Pneumatic spreader (12m-24m) mounted	4500 - 26000
trailed	8000 - 20,000
Contractors charges	**£/ha**
Fertiliser application (380 kg/ha)	8.90
(exclusive of material and haulage)	

Source: AB.C.

HEALTH

WEEDS

Control of weeds is necessary to reduce adverse effects on yield, quality and ease of harvesting. Neither peas nor beans are very competitive in their early stages of growth so weeds must be removed as early as possible. Perennial weeds (e.g. couch) should be controlled before sowing peas or beans.

Weed Control

Crop	Important weeds	Control strategy
Peas and Spring Beans Knotgrass	Annual broad leaved weeds, especially polygonums i.e. knotgrass, black bindweed and redshank; wild oats	pre-emergence herbicides preferred; follow-up with post-emergence sprays if necessary Redshank
Winter Beans	Annual grass weeds, especially wild oats and blackgrass, cleavers	soil residual herbicides available; follow-up herbicides should not be necessary

Warning: Check varietal tolerance of peas to herbicides.

DISEASES

Diseases reduce yield and quality. The latter is especially important with peas for human consumption. Weed control is an important aspect of disease control as weeds can carry over diseases through the rotation. Successful weed control should ensure even maturity, possibly avoiding the use of a desiccant.

The basis of good disease control is a wide rotation (no more than 1 year in 5) and the use of healthy seed with a suitable seed treatment. Sprays are most likely to pay in a wet season.

HEALTH

Disease Control

Crop	Important diseases	Disease type	Control strategy
Peas	Downy mildew, Ascochyta, Damping-off, Pea-wilt Fusarium, Sclerotinia Botrytis	Fungus	seed treatment, rotation, *choose less susceptible varieties
	Common pea mosaic virus	**Virus**	**apply aphicide**
	Pea early browning virus	Virus	apply nematicide
	Bacterial blight *	**Bacteria**	**no treatment (some varities less susceptible)**
Spring and Beans	Chocolate spot	Fungus	apply fungicide sprays, especially winter beans.
	Aschochyta	**Fungus**	**Seed Treatment**
	Leaf roll virus	Virus	apply aphicide

 * This is a notifiable disease and growers suspecting this disease is present in their crops must, by law, contact the Ministry of Agriculture as soon as possible.

PESTS

The severity of pest incidence is affected significantly by soil type, crop rotation and weather conditions. Pests reduce yield and quality but **routine spraying should be avoided** as it may give rise to **pesticide resistance** and it's too expensive anyway!

HEALTH

Crop	Important pests	Control strategy
Peas and Beans	Pea and bean weevil	granular insecticide
	Leatherjackets (may follow grass)	in seedbed
	Slugs	slug pellets
	Aphids	aphicide sprays
	Nematodes	rotation, granular nematicide in extreme circumstances
Peas only	Pea moth	insecticide sprays
	Pea midge	

Black bean aphid

LEGAL ASPECTS

Food And Environment Protection Act (F.E.P.A.)

Main provisions:

i   Sprayer operators born after 1965 must have a certificate of competence. All sprayer contractors must have the certificate, regardless of age.

ii   Pesticides must be applied in strict accordance with manufacturers instruction.

iii   Only approved tank mixes may be used.

iv   Observe the required "harvest interval" i.e. minimum time between spraying and harvesting.

v   Do not exceed recommended rates.

vi   Avoid spray drift.

vii   Store chemicals in suitable secure building which can retain spillage in the event of a fire.

viii   Use waste contractors to dispose of excess spray and empty containers.

ix   Avoid pollution of watercourses.

x   Minimise harm to wildlife.

xi   Operators should wear at least the minimum protective clothing required for the pesticide being used.

HEALTH

C.O.S.H.H.

Control of Substances Hazardous to Health. A further development of the Health and Safety at Work Act. It is the responsibility of the employer to make an adequate assessment of the risks from hazardous materials, (including pesticides, micro-organisms, dust etc.) and decide on the control measures to prevent exposure.

EQUIPMENT COSTS

Sprayer Equipment	Detail	Width	Cost Range £
Mounted on tractor	200-400 litre	6-12m	900 - 2200
Mounted on tractor	600-800 litre	6-18m	1500 - 10000
Trailed	500-2500 litre	12-24m	5500 - 21500
Trailed	3000-4100 litre	18-36m	14500 - 44000
Self-propelled sprayer /fertiliser distributor	800-3000 litre	12-24m	14000 - 61000
Contractors Charges			**£/ha**
Standard spraying	225l/ha		9.90

Source: A.B.C.

HARVESTING

AIMS

To harvest the crop in such a way as to minimise damage to the sample and crop losses.

PRE-HARVEST TREATMENT

If one crop is ripening unevenly and is to be harvested dry, it is advisable to use a desiccant spray (see for timing). The crop may be combine harvested 7 - 10 days after the use of a desiccant.

TIMING CRITERIA

Visual Assessment

Crop	Foliage condition	Seed condition
Dried peas	Foliage dead	Seed wrinkled and hard
Field beans	Pods and stems black	Seed brown and hard

Vining crops must be assessed by an experienced fieldsman who uses a device called a "Tenderometer" to assist him.

Moisture Content

This is the most accurate test of maturity for dried crops. The farmer is looking for a moisture content of less than 25%, but the nearer 15% the better.

Drier crops, (15% moisture content) are easier to harvest but in a wet season waiting for the crop to dry can result in unacceptable losses due to pod shatter, and for peas intended for human consumption, unacceptable levels of staining.

HARVESTING

Quality requirements vary according to market outlet. For **feed** crops sample quality is not such an important issue. For **seed** crops and crops destined for **human** consumption the following damage should be avoided:

Dried crops

cracking

waste and admixture

stain, bleaching

Vining crops

specific requirements dependent on processor

POST HARVEST CARE

Vining crops are removed from the farm as soon as they are harvested. Dried crops may be stored for several months but must be dried down to 14% moisture content (for long term storage) to prevent deterioration.

Drying may be achieved:

either in **bulk** by

i   on floor (store has undercrop ventilation) or

ii   in bin (again ventilated)

or by **high temperature** drying, through

i   a continuous flow drier or

ii   a batch drier

Warning

Avoid excessive drying temperatures as quality may suffer. Drying legumes is a slow process.

STRAW DISPOSAL

Dried pea and bean straw can either be spread and ploughed in or baled and fed to cattle.

Vining crop residues are normally ploughed in. This operation helps to prevent the carry-over of diseases in both dried and vining crops.

STORAGE MANAGEMENT

- ☞ Clean store before use.

- ☞ Store only clean, dry, cooled peas/beans.

- ☞ Monitor temperature and moisture content throughout the heap on a regular basis.

- ☞ Any increase in temperature or moisture content should be investigated immediately.

Possible problems include mould growth and bean beetle. Mouldy peas should be dried and ventilated. Pest infestations will require fumigation (usually a contractors job). Sampling for quality is normally undertaken by a representative of the purchaser. The farmer should keep a sample of his own for independent analysis in the event of any dispute.

LEGAL ASPECTS

Under the Control of Substances Hazardous to Health (C.O.S.H.H.) potential hazards should be assessed and minimised. Mould and dust associated with harvesting, drying and storage should be monitored and preventative measures taken. Breathing apparatus should be provided where necessary.

The Health and Safety at Work Act states that both employees and employers are responsible for safety in the work place and safety defects and unsafe practice should be reported.

HARVESTING

HARVESTING, DRYING AND STORAGE COSTS

Equipment	Detail	£
Combine harvester	90 - 111kW 3.6 - 4.9m	50000 - 70000
Baler	small, rectangular bales	7500 - 9500
Drier		£/t
capital cost/t of hourly rate annual fixed costs	10 - 40 tonnes/hour depreciation/interest/t	1500 - 2350 4.50 - 6.70
Storage		
capital cost very variable depending on building		30 - 150

Source: A.B.C.

CONTRACTORS CHARGES

Operation	£/ha
Combining harvesting peas	98.85
Combining harvesting beans	74.15
Drying peas and beans down to 14% moisture from 26% moisture content: from 18% moisture content:	£/t 18.00 - 18.75 9.25 - 9.60
Storage - per week	0.26 - 0.32
Handling - to store only	4.00 - 4.25

Source: A.B.C.

PERFORMANCE

KEY ASSESSMENT QUESTIONS

Profitability is optimised if a lucrative market outlet is identified, and a variety chosen to meet that need. Inputs should be used sensibly, up to a level where further use would not produce a return sufficient to cover costs. Consider:

- ☞ expected market outlet
- ☞ variety choice and sowing date
- ☞ crop yield, price and any premium obtained
- ☞ use of inputs including establishment and harvesting
- ☞ crop conditioning and storage techniques
- ☞ timing of sale
- ☞ use of production/marketing contracts
- ☞ reason for choice of vining peas / dried peas / winter beans / spring beans
- ☞ level of hectareage payment

PHYSICAL PERFORMANCE

Pea National Average Yields

Wet weather, soil compaction and difficult harvest conditions all severely depress pea yields, for example in 1985 and 1987.

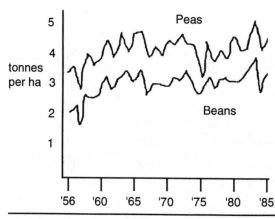

Peas have developed the reputation of being a rich man's crop - in some years even the very best farmers lose money through no fault of their own. Of course the profitability of pea growing must be viewed long term. In the drier parts of the UK the crop has performed very well indeed over the last decade.

PERFORMANCE

Bean Yields

Bean yields also have a reputation of being inconsistent. This was due to a lack of knowledge of the crop. If plant populations per square metre are within the optimum range, the crop is planted at the correct time, and kept clear of weed, pest and disease attack, yields can be surprisingly inconsistent. Beans are less prone to yield loss in wet conditions than peas.

Average bean yields over the last decade have been 3.2 tonnes per hectare, identical to the average pea yield. Sale price per tonne of beans is lower than peas, but so are the costs of production, resulting in similar levels of profitability. As mentioned in Environment (🌲), soil type should dictate which legume crop to go for.

GROSS MARGIN ANALYSIS

	Output £ Per Ha			
	Vining Peas	Protein Peas	Winter Field Beans	Field Beans Spring
Yields (t/ha)		including £360/ha area payment		
4.5 t/ha @ £185/t	835			
3.7 t/ha @£142/t		710		
3.6 t/ha @£87.5/t			675	
3.4 t/ha @£87.5/t				660
	Variable Costs (£/ha)			
Seed				
250 kg @48p/kg	120			
235 kg @47p/kg		110		
190 kg @28p/kg			55	
220 kg @28p/kg				60
Fertilizer				
0N:25P:40K kg	15	15		
0N:40P:45K kg			12.5	12.5
Contracting/harvesting	248			
Transport	101			
Chemicals	50	90	62.5	52.5
Total Variable Costs	**534**	**215**	**130**	**125**
Gross Margin (£/ha)	**301**	**495**	**545**	**535**

Source: J. Nix 1994

OUTSIDER'S GUIDE

PERFORMANCE

GROSS MARGIN SENSITIVITY ANALYSIS

Example: Field Beans - Spring

Assuming constant variable costs of £172 per hectare and an area payment of £378/ha:

		Yield Tonnes per hectare							
		2.8	3.1	3.4	3.7	4.0	4.3	4.6	4.9
Gross Margins	£/ha								
	133	578	618	658	698	738	778	817	857
Price £ per	136	586	627	668	709	750	790	831	872
tonne	139	595	637	678	720	762	803	845	887
	142	603	646	688	731	774	816	859	901
	145	612	612	699	**742**	786	829	873	916
	148	620	620	709	753	798	842	886	931
	151	628	628	719	764	810	855	900	946
	154	637	637	729	775	822	868	914	960
	157	645	692	739	787	834	881	928	975

Source: A.B.C.

FIXED COSTS ELEMENTS

Fixed costs are, by definition, all the costs of a farm business that cannot be allocated to individual enterprises as Variable Costs.

The costs on the following pages are approximate guide figures intended for budgets currently being prepared. They show the relative fixed costs for different farming systems of various farm sizes that are going concerns. They should not be used for analysis purposes, i.e. compared with historical data

New farm businesses may have Rent figures 40% to 70% higher than those indicated.

Cost Categories

Labour	includes all full time labour costs, an estimated value for the manual work carried out by the farmer and his family, plus general casual labour

PERFORMANCE

Depreciation	calculated on a replacement cost basis
Contract	used for general work only such as hedging or ditching
Rent	actual rent or rental value including imputed rent on the net costs of improvements
Land maintenance	traditional tenants' repairs plus landlord type repairs carried out by tenants under a full repairing tenancy
Sundries	overheads of the business such as insurance, professional fees, office and telephone, subscriptions etc., but excluding interest charges

TYPICAL FIXED COSTS

	under 120ha	120-240ha	over 240ha
Mainly cereals at least 70% under combinable crops	577	537 *	480

Fixed Cost Components

*As an example, costs for this size group are shown below:

	120-240ha
Labour	160
Depreciation	95
Repairs, Tax, Ins	50
Fuel & Electricity	32
General contract	20
Rent & Rates	120
Land maintenance	20
Fixed costs sundries	40
Total fixed costs	**537**

Source: A.B.C.

Actual fixed costs vary dramatically between farming businesses, even though they may look similar. At least 80% of farms borrow money for part, if not all of the year. If substantial borrowings are combined with rental payments, overall fixed costs will be £550/ha or more.

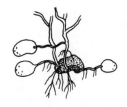

THE
OUTSIDER'S GUIDE
to
MAINCROP POTATOES

1995 Edition

OUTSIDER'S GUIDE

INTRODUCTION

Potatoes were first domesticated in South America and by the time the Spaniards arrived in the 16th century they had already spread considerably. Plant breeders today still return to South America in search of new genetic material from the many wild potato strains that still exist.

On a protein and calorie per hectare production basis the potato is ahead of maize, rice and wheat. To feed the ever-increasing world population, the potato crop seems to have a secure future. Production statistics on a world basis are unreliable although North America remains the leading producer.

EU PRODUCTION STATISTICS

European Union Potato Production '93

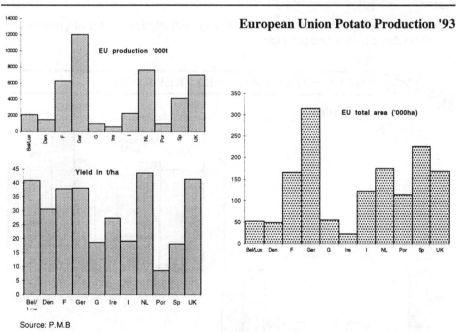

Source: P.M.B

Despite the relatively low value and bulky nature of the crop imports into the UK, particularly of processing potatoes, pose a serious threat. France, the Netherlands and Belgium all produce potato crops in excess of their domestic requirements.

Traditional first early imports from Egypt, the Canary Islands, Spain and Greece etc. will continue due to their obvious climatic advantages.

PRODUCTION

UK PRODUCTION TRENDS

The UK Crop continues to pass into the hands of larger but increasingly specialised growers. Within the next ten years, it is estimated that less than 1,000 growers will produce 50% of the national crop.

As average potato yields increase, the area planted will decline unless additional markets can be exploited to absorb the surplus. The crop will increasingly be grown on lighter soil types, but with irrigation to improve yield potential and skin quality.

An ever increasing proportion of the crop will be washed and pre-packed and then sold through supermarket outlets rather than the traditional corner shop. Overall potato quality will improve in response to customer demands and by necessity in the face of growing imports.

UK consumption per head is actually increasing, probably due to improving quality and increasing diversity of potato products.

THE UK POTATO INDUSTRY - KEY FACTS

Production

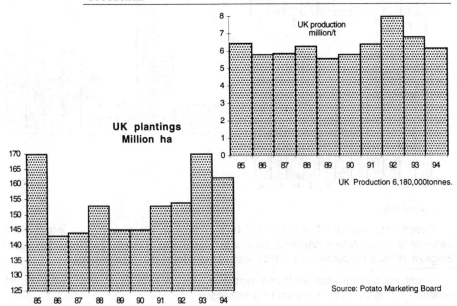

UK Production 6,180,000tonnes.

Source: Potato Marketing Board

OUTSIDER'S GUIDE

PRODUCTION TRENDS AND CYCLES

The UK Potato hectarage is strictly governed by the **Potato Marketing Board** (P.M.B.) quota system introduced in 1958. Prior to this, favourable seasons produced higher than average yields forcing down prices and forcing some growers out of production.

In subsequent years, reduced plantings forced up prices giving rise to a cyclical pattern favouring neither producers or consumers alike.

Although the hectareage is now controlled and does not vary greatly, yields and therefore prices can fluctuate according to season. In 1975 and 1976, two successive drought years, UK potato production was reduced from six to four million tonnes.

Almost 50% of the UK maincrop is now irrigated which should greatly reduce such marked fluctuations.

Main Growing Regions For Potatoes

PRODUCTION

Why Grow Potatoes?

- ☛ Undoubtedly the major factor is profitability (considered further in)
- ☛ Guaranteed market. The P.M.B. provides a support mechanism
- ☛ Excellent weed, pest and disease break for other crops following
- ☛ Good grass weed control possible
- ☛ Spreads the farm workload more evenly throughout the year
- ☛ Provides an opportunity for farm-gate sales

KEY ASSESSMENT QUESTIONS

	Maincrop	Earlies
Production level (t/ha)	40	20
Price/tonne (£)	70	120
Output (£)	2800	2400
Total variable costs (£)	1717	1359
Gross margin £/ha	**1083**	**1041**

Source: A.B.C.

FACTORS AFFECTING POTATO PROFITABILITY

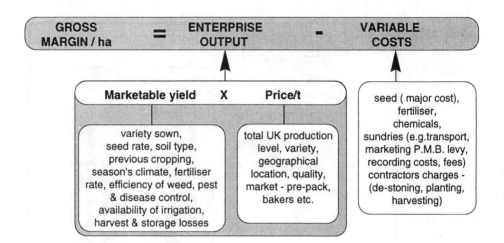

GROSS MARGIN / ha	=	ENTERPRISE OUTPUT	−	VARIABLE COSTS

Marketable yield X **Price/t**

variety sown, seed rate, soil type, previous cropping, season's climate, fertiliser rate, efficiency of weed, pest & disease control, availability of irrigation, harvest & storage losses

total UK production level, variety, geographical location, quality, market - pre-pack, bakers etc.

seed (major cost), fertiliser, chemicals, sundries (e.g.transport, marketing P.M.B. levy, recording costs, fees) contractors charges - (de-stoning, planting, harvesting)

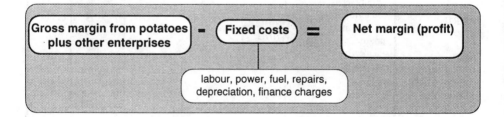

Gross margin from potatoes plus other enterprises − **Fixed costs** = **Net margin (profit)**

labour, power, fuel, repairs, depreciation, finance charges

PRODUCTION

THE PRODUCTION CYCLE - MAINCROP POTATOES

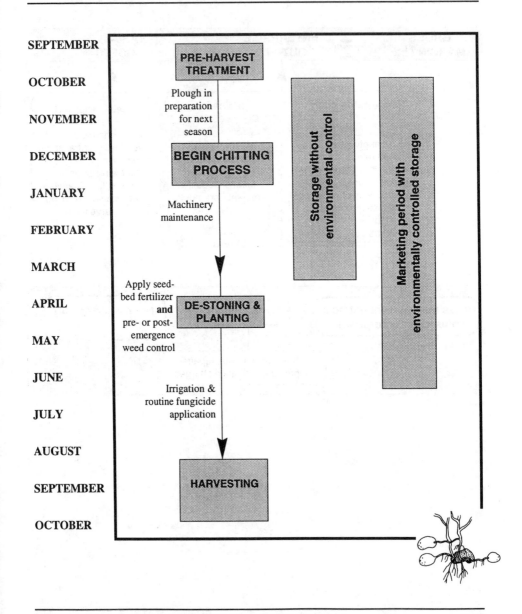

Month	Process	Activity
SEPTEMBER	**PRE-HARVEST TREATMENT**	
OCTOBER		Plough in preparation for next season
NOVEMBER		
DECEMBER	**BEGIN CHITTING PROCESS**	
JANUARY		Machinery maintenance
FEBRUARY		
MARCH		Apply seed-bed fertilizer **and** pre- or post-emergence weed control
APRIL	**DE-STONING & PLANTING**	
MAY		
JUNE		Irrigation & routine fungicide application
JULY		
AUGUST		
SEPTEMBER	**HARVESTING**	
OCTOBER		

Storage without environmental control

Marketing period with environmentally controlled storage

MAIN PRODUCTS

i Human consumption:

Ware	Potatoes sold whole e.g. through wholesale markets, greengrocers, farm-gate sales etc.
Processing	Exacting variety and quality standards for crisps, chips (french fries), dehydration, canning
Pre-packing	Exacting quality standard. Rapidly expanding (supermarket sector trade).

ii Stockfeed: Excess potatoes or 'Chats' too small or of too a low quality for human consumption.

iii Seed: Must meet stringent legal standards for health, purity and vigour.

By-products: Starch extracts for glues, custards and for production of glucose and alcohol, citric acid.

QUALITY STANDARDS

Ware

Samples must be free from soil, stones, adhering plant growth and any other extraneous matter.

Grading must remove the following: shrivelled or wizened tubers, diseased or affected by rots, covered by common scab over more than 25% of surface, affected by greening, bruised or discoloured internally, damaged by wireworms, slugs or other pests or by frost, mis-shaped or affected by growth cracks, secondary growth or hollow heart, tainted, affected by growth shoots.

Also quality specifies undersize and oversize potatoes which must be graded out:-

Ware grade - Above the 85mm riddle and below the 45mm riddle.

Small grade - Above the maximum riddle and below the minimum riddle within a 25mm size range selected for the grade.

Large grade - Below the 25mm riddle.

Tolerance - The permitted tolerance of faults to 5% may be interpreted as 1.25 g in 25 kg. **Ware potatoes sold in 25 kg bags must carry the producer's number in case of any quality complaint.**

French Fries

Medium to large sized tubers, over 45 mm with shallow eyes and regular shape, cream or white flesh, no blemishes, free from internal bruising, disease, cracking and greening, specific gravity over 1.080 (20% dry matter), reducing sugar content below 0.25% and no tendency to turn grey or black after cooking.

MARKETING

Crisps

Uniform regular shaped medium sized tubers over 40 mm with clean skin with shallow eyes, free from internal bruising disease and greening, specific gravity over 1.085 (21% dry matter), with reducing sugar content below 0.20% and preferably below 0.10%.

Pre-Pack

As for ware but specified varieties only, even size and good skin finish.

MARKET PREFERRED VARIETIES

Market	Varieties
Crisping	Record, Saturna, Lady Rosetta
Chipping (french fries)	Pentland Dell, Russet Burbank, Maris Piper
Pre-packing	Cara, Maris Piper, Pentland Squire, Estima, Wilja, Romano, Desiree, King Edward, Nadine
Canning	Maris Peer
Baking	Cara, Pentland Squire, Estima, Marfona

Total Area Planted By Producers With Leading Varieties 1993

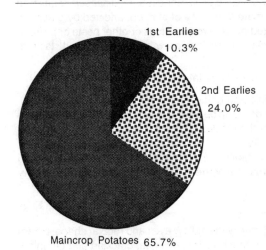

1st Earlies 10.3%

2nd Earlies 24.0%

Maincrop Potatoes 65.7%

Varieties accounting for 70% of total percentage grown in order of importance:

1st earlies	Maris Bard
	Pentland Javelin
	Rocket
2nd earlies	Estima
	Wilja
	Marfona
Maincrop	Maris Piper
	Record
	Cara
	Pentland Dell
	Desiree

SOURCE: P.M.B. Potato Statistics Bulletin (NIAB)

MARKETING

UK POTATO CONSUMPTION

Annual Consumption

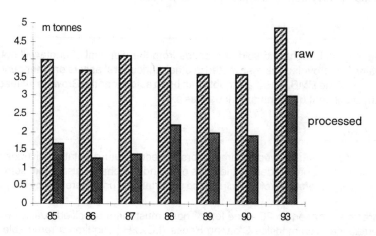

Source: P.M.B. Annual Report & Accounts 1992

P.M.B. LEVIES AND QUOTAS

The Potato Marketing Board

P.M.B. - The Potato Marketing Board is a statutory organisation with which all producers and merchants must register their production (and be allocated an area quota), or be licensed to buy and sell potatoes. The P.M.B. currently specify standards and organise price support. With the winding up of the PMB there is likely to be greater uncertainty.

By limiting the area of potatoes grown the P.M.B. controls, to an extent at least, production and pricing, in the interests of both producers and consumers. In return for the levy paid on an area basis, the P.M.B. is able to fund administration of the scheme, develop marketing strategies and provide a minimum guaranteed price for producers. In the past intervention support was partly funded by government, but this has now been withdrawn.

1994 Quota

The 1995 quota has been set at 97.5% of basic area. A growers basic area is the average annual area of land under potatoes during the 3 previous seasons i.e. 91, 92 and 93. Effectively, growers are forced to reduce their potato acreage accordingly.

MARKETING

Levy

This is set at £ 12/ha for earlies lifted before 30 June. After this date: £ 48/ha (see ). Growers exceeding their quota area are liable to a fine (excess levy) of £856/ha. The PMB has reduced the levy from £750/ha to £200/ha in 1995.

Quota

Quota may be bought and sold. Proceeds from the disposal of quota will not attract capital gains tax provided it is re-invested in other agricultural assets or other quota. Due to the demise of the PMB, little if any quota has been sold recently. Growers instead prefer to rent any additional quota on an annual basis.

Potato Futures

The futures market is used by processors to secure future potato deliveries at fixed prices. Farmers, market traders (Nine Elms etc.) and merchants also make some use of the market. It is a useful way of reducing price uncertainty if used carefully by the producer or user.

Contracts are based on 20 tonne lots. These must meet specified quality standards. The International Commodities Clearing House (I.C.C.H.) requires a returnable margin (deposit) for ware potatoes of £200 per contract.

All trading must be carried out through brokers at the Baltic Exchange London. Delivery months -September, October, November, February, March, April, May, June.

UK AVERAGE PRODUCER PRICES

1993/94 Seasons And Supply

The '93 potato harvest was affected by heavy prolonged rain during September and October and delayed lifting and lead to fears of serious field & store losses. Some crops were lost through flooding and others damaged by frost. However, the potato crops harvested give reasonable high yields and prices remained low. In 1994, although many crops were irrigated, the mid summer drought affected yield. The reduced plantings and yields have reduced supplies and consequently prices are very high.

ENVIRONMENT

PREFERRED ENVIRONMENT

Climate

Ideally the crop requires the following conditions:

- ☛ dry spring for good seedbed preparation
- ☛ ample sunshine and moisture during the growing season
- ☛ dry from late September into October to enable easier harvesting
- ☛ maincrop and 2nd earlies generally in the drier eastern counties. Earlies in the South, S. West and S. Wales where early warm springs enable early planting
- ☛ seed potatoes grown on high ground especially Scotland where colder conditions discourage aphids and therefore aphid transmitted virus diseases e.g. virus leaf roll.

Soils

Light (sands)	Medium (loams)	Heavy (clays)
Ideal for seedbed preparation	**Ideal**	Poor compacted, cloddy seedbeds
Fail to hold moisture therefore irrigation essential	Moisture - retentive yet well-drained	Retain moisture therefore irrigation not necessary
Can lead to increased bruising damage at harvest	Good retention of nutrients Stone free	Difficult harvesting conditions when wet.
	Level for efficient use of large machinery	

Organic (Peaty) Soils

Well suited, however, high nitrogen content can be a disadvantage.

DRAINAGE

Well drained soils essential, excess water can:

i delay planting and establishment

ii encourage disease e.g. powdery scab

ENVIRONMENT

   iii result in poor seedbed preparation, possible clod formation

   iv result in poor rooting and lower yields

   v   encourage more slug damage particularly in susceptible varieties

   vi result in difficult harvesting conditions.

IRRIGATION

In dry seasons, 1975 and 1976 in particular, and more recently 1988 to 1991, potatoes have been particularly responsive to irrigation producing yield increases of up to 30%. The general move to lighter, less moisture-retentive soil types necessitates irrigation to produce satisfactory yields.

ROTATIONS

Rotations were historically 1 year in 7 to prevent the build up of potato cyst nematode (P.C.N.). Due to increasing specialism and larger potato acreages being grown by individual farmers maincrop may be grown on a one in four rotation.

Potatoes traditionally follow 2 cereal crops to provide a suitable break. Following potatoes, winter wheat is usually grown or alternatively, a spring cereal.

Example Rotation

Year	
1	Winter wheat
2	Winter wheat
3	Maincrop Potatoes
4	Winter wheat or peas (protein)
5	Spring barley

N.B. 15% Set-Aside must now be included in all arable rotations possibly to replace the 2nd wheat or spring barley in the example rotation.

MAINCROP POTATO ESTABLISHMENT

1 Chitting

Chitting is physiological ageing of the tuber to encourage the development of stems using a combination of heat and light. The advantages are: earlier plant emergence; earlier tuber initiation; earlier harvesting, when soils are warmer and drier. Finally, chitting also helps to produce higher yields.

ENVIRONMENT

2 Seedbed Preparation

Stone and clod separation techniques are increasingly used. Advantages are that it: allows the use of unmanned harvesters; faster harvester work rates; better shaped tubers and increased marketable yield.

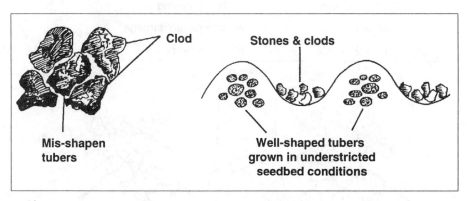

Aim:

To produce a tilth free from clods and stones, sufficient to form a ridge to protect tubers adequately throughout the growing season.

In Spring, use straight rather than curved tines which drag up unweathered material. Avoid compaction beneath the ridge and do not plough light land too early as this leads to "slumping".

3 Planting Date

Planting date will depend on type of potato, soil condition and potato physiological age. Earlies are normally planted between February and March and Main crops from beginning of April.

If well sprouted tubers are planted into cold wet soils, several varieties can be affected by "coiled sprout or little potato disorder".

4 Seed Size

Seed potatoes are usually graded 35 x 55 mm i.e. they pass through a 55 mm riddle (sieve) but over a 35 mm one. Use of small seed 20-30mm could reduce seed costs.

ENVIRONMENT

5 Row Width

Wider row widths provide the following advantages without any reduction in yield:

	i shallower seedbed cultivations
30" = 762 mm	ii less greening
34" = 863 mm	iii less potato damage
36" = 914 mm	iv fewer clods

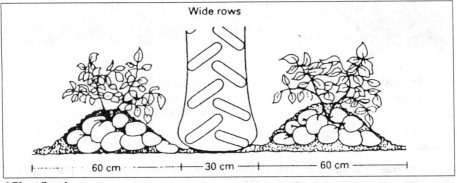

Wide rows

|←----- 60 cm -----→|←---- 30 cm ----→|←----- 60 cm -----→|

6 Plant Spacing

This is largely determined by seed rate. Usually plants are between 170 and 400 mm apart. For example for **Pentland Squire** which produces over-size tubers you need to plant closer together, while **King Edward,** which produces many small tubers, are planted further apart.

7 Seed Rate Determination

The following information is required: seed count i.e. tuber number/50 kg bag; the seed cost : ware value ratio; variety and the optimum plant population (O.P.P.).

e.g. Variety **Cara.**

Seed count 800/50 kg bag.   Seed cost: ware value ratio estimated as 2.5:1

Optimum plant population according to seed count and cost = 51,200 (available from A.D.A.S. Leaflet P653 seed rate for potatoes grown as maincrop).

$$\text{Seed rate in tonnes per ha} = \frac{\text{O.P.P.}^{**}}{\text{Seed count} \times 20} = \frac{51,200}{800 \times 20^*}$$

Thus the seed rate = 3.2 t/ha   (* 20 x 50 kg = 1 tonne.)

** Optimum Plant Population

THE POTATO PRODUCTION CYCLE

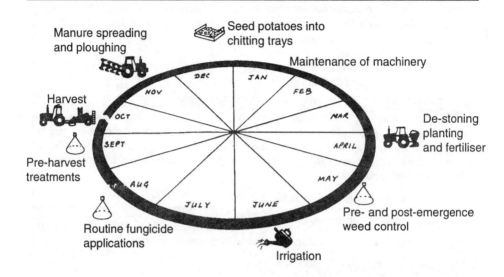

Manure spreading and ploughing

Seed potatoes into chitting trays

Maintenance of machinery

Harvest

De-stoning planting and fertiliser

Pre-harvest treatments

Pre- and post-emergence weed control

Routine fungicide applications

Irrigation

THE POTATO GROWTH CYCLE

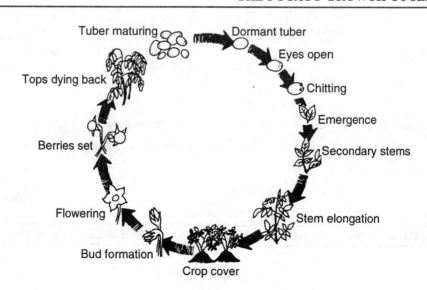

Tuber maturing

Dormant tuber

Eyes open

Tops dying back

Chitting

Emergence

Berries set

Secondary stems

Flowering

Stem elongation

Bud formation

Crop cover

GROWTH STAGES

1 Chitting.

- ensures earlier emergence ⎤ growth pattern of
- earlier tuber initiation ⎟ crop advanced
- earlier senescence (die-back) ⎦
- usually a higher yield
- chemical seed treatment e.g. Rizolex Vs. Black scurf and stem canker.

2 Planting.

Planting too early into cold damp soils can encourage Blackleg diseases and a physiological disorder known as "coiled - sprout" when the chits or sprouts coil around the mother tuber rather than grow upwards to form stems. This disorder is most common in the variety Pentland Dell.

The majority of fertiliser is applied at this stage.

3 Encourage early emergence.

To maximise the interception of sunlight energy to produce optimum yield.

3 & 4 Apply herbicides to control weeds.

Possibly top-dress with additional nitrogen, especially on irrigated sandy soils.

5 The start of tuber initiation. Irrigation to control potato scab at this point.

6 Plants meeting within the row.

This creates a micro-climate beneath the foliage. Warm, humid conditions encourage potato blight. Commence blight-spray programme at this point, and continue up to plant yellowing stage.

Aim to achieve full ground cover by the longest day - 21st June.

7, 8 & 9 Continue to irrigate according to soil moisture deficit (S.M.D.)

10 Pre-harvest treatments to ensure skin set before harvest e.g.

Application of sulphuric acid.

Desiccation with "Reglone", or "Challenge".

Mechanical defoliation, usually after desiccation.

11 Commence harvest ensuring skins are set and mechanical damage is minimised.

NUTRITION

NUTRIENT REQUIREMENTS

Acidity - pH

Potatoes tolerate relatively low pH conditions, 5.5 or above on mineral soils and 5.0 on peats. High pH encourages common scab therefore avoid applications of lime immediately prior to potatoes.

Farm Yard Manure (FYM)

Large applications of FYM are often made in the previous Autumn to:

> **a Improve the soil structure**
>
> **b Improve the soils water-holding capacity**
>
> **c Provide an additional source of nutrients although frequently not considered in overall N, P and K requirement.**

Application Rates

Soil type		N, P, K or Mg Index	
		0 kg/ha	2 kg/ha
All mineral soils	Nitrogen (N)	220	100
	Phosphate (P_2O_5)	350	250
	Potash (K_2O)	350	250
Peaty soils except moss soils	Nitrogen (N)	130	50
	Phosphate (P_2O_5)	350	250
	Potash (K_2O)	350	250
Organic, moss & warp soils	Nitrogen (N)	180	80
	Phosphate (P_2O_5)	350	250
	Potash (K_2O)	350	250
All soils	Magnesium (Mg)	165	Nil

Source: A.D.A.S. Fertiliser Recommendations

Note:- In the majority of instances, potatoes will be grown on soils of N index 0, and P and K index 2 to 3. If growing second earlies the nitrogen rate can be reduced by 50kg/ha.

NUTRITION

Phosphate and Potash response curves are relatively flat i.e. at high levels of nutrient application yields continue to increase but only slowly.

After high levels of P and K application, any remaining nutrients will benefit later crops in the rotation.

Recent evidence suggest that the variety **Cara**, which produces a particularly vigorous top growth requires less nitrogen, probably 150 N/ha at most. Growers placing fertilizer in 2 bands just beneath the seed tuber, should be able to cut fertilizer rates by 20-30%.

METHOD OF APPLICATION

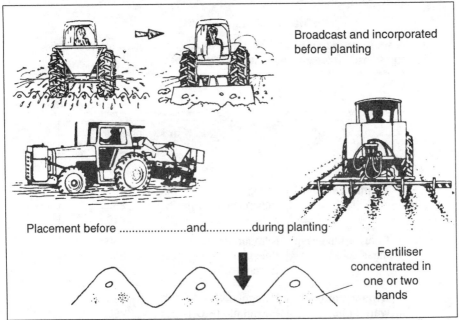

Broadcast and incorporated before planting

Placement before ....and..............during planting

Fertiliser concentrated in one or two bands

Fertiliser placed close to, but not in contact with developing sprouts, is generally more efficient. Avoid placing more than 250 kg/ha of Na and K, especially in dry seasons and on mineral soils.

Such placed fertiliser is often in liquid form and applied at the time of planting.

NUTRITION

Application Timing

Nitrogen

Generally, apply all at planting or just before. On sandy, irrigated soils, apply half at planting and half at tuber initiation, to reduce the danger of leaching. Potatoes are not particularly efficient in using applied nitrogen and any residual nitrogen left after the crop may be prone to leaching.

Phosphorus

Apply all phosphate in spring using water soluble types.

Potassium

Apply some K the previous autumn especially the less soluble types. Potash helps to reduce tuber damage.

Potatoes For Processing

E.g. crisps and french fry processing.

Generally apply rates as for ware production. Excessive nitrogen can reduce tuber dry matter content leading to rejection for crisping purposes. Using potassium sulphate can increase tuber dry matter content, desirable for processing.

Trace Elements

Manganese (Mn) deficiency can occur on organic soils with a pH over 6.0.

Foliar manganese sprays should give a yield benefit.

NUTRIENT DEFICIENCY SYMPTOMS

Nutrient	Deficiency symptoms
N	pale green foliage, early senescence
P,K,Mg	not seen unless nutrient index is zero
Mn	pale younger leaves. Black/brown spots particularly on underside of leaves

NUTRITION

POTATO GROWTH REGULATORS

 Considerable manipulation of the crop is possible without growth regulators e.g. varying within row spacings to influence tuber size. Only one growth regulator, Fazor, is commercially available which claims to suppress the production of small tubers which might otherwise become volunteers in subsequent crops and also to suppress in-store sprouting.

TYPICAL POTATO FERTILISERS AND COSTS:

	N%	P%	K%	£/t	
Compounds	17	17	17	118-128	
	15	15	21	115-125	
	0	24	24	95-108	
	34.5	-	-	95-110	
Straights	-	-	50%K	155-170	(Sulphate of Potash)
	-	-	60%K	100 - 115	(Muriate of Potash)
	-	46%	-	115-125	(Triple Superphosphate)
Trace	Kieserite (16% Mg)			£105 -£115	

Source: ABC

TYPICAL EQUIPMENT COSTS

Item	Detail	Cost range £'000
Power harrow	3-8m	7 - 21
Heavy cultivator	3-4m	3 - 6
Straw incorporator (disks)	3-4m	5.3 - 11.5
Potato ridger	4 row	2.3 - 2.5
Planter for chitted seed	4 row	6.5 - 15.5
Stone clod separator	2 row	13.0-18.0
Trailed fertilizer spreader	12-20m	8-20

Satisfactory weed, pest and disease control ensures optimum yield, the required tuber quality and easier harvesting.

WEEDS AND WEED CONTROL

Important Considerations

Potatoes are particularly sensitive to yield loss due to weed competition. An effective weed-control programme is therefore an essential part of good crop management. It takes the crop several weeks to meet between the row and smother out weed growth.

Weed infested crops are also particularly difficult to harvest.

Weeds compete for nutrients and moisture during key growth stages leading to both reduced yield and quality. In addition, weedy crops attract more pests e.g. slugs and cutworms, further reducing tuber quality.

Weeds left uncontrolled, will contribute to the soil's weed seed bank.

Major Weeds

Principally Spring germinators:

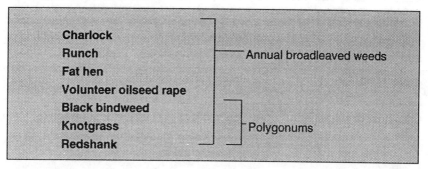

Charlock
Runch
Fat hen
Volunteer oilseed rape — Annual broadleaved weeds
Black bindweed
Knotgrass — Polygonums
Redshank

Volunteer cereals — Annual grass weeds(A.G.W.)
Spring germinating wild oats

Couch — Perennial grass weed. (P.G.W.)

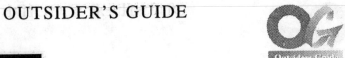

HEALTH

CONTROL STRATEGIES

Cultural vs **Chemical**	
(i.e. inter-row cultivation) (herbicide)	
or, a Combination?	
risk further clod formation	pesticide cost
lose moisture	beware possible plant damage
possibly physical plant damage	variable effectiveness
may encourage further weed seed germination	
cannot be used if stones and clods already separated	

Herbicide Choice Criteria

Current/expected weed flora	beware of varietal susceptibility with certain post-emergence products.
Soil type influences	herbicide type (on lighter soils, herbicides leach).
Application rate	may vary according to the soil type.
Crop growth stage i.e.	during seedbed preparation or pre-planting.
	pre-emergence; pre-planting treatments must be incorporated quickly.
	post emergence - delayed spraying, even with selective herbicides can depress yields.
Cost effectiveness	

Note: Soil acting residual types require moisture.

200   **MAINCROP POTATOES**   1995

HEALTH

PESTS AND PEST CONTROL

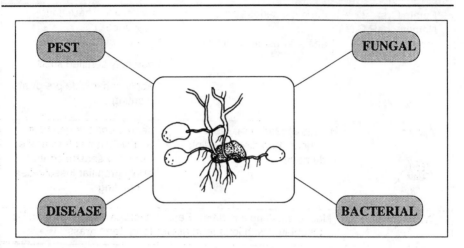

Pest Damage

This happens by:

root feeding	leading to foliar wilting and yield reduction e.g. potato cyst nematode
tuber damage	leading to rejection at grading e.g. wireworms, cutworms and slugs
foliar damage	e.g. COLORADO BEETLE (a notifiable pest which could become established in the UK after the Channel Tunnel opening)
diseases carriers	aphids act as vectors, or carriers of viral diseases e.g. virus leaf roll

HEALTH

Pest	Significance	Control
Potato Cyst Nematode (P.C.N.) (cyst eel worm)	the most serious pest easily transmitted in soil	test soil for nematode presence grow resistant varieties use only certified seed apply nematicide pre or at planting
Aphids	virus spread is far more serious than direct feeding damage	seed crops are grown in relatively aphid free areas. For early season control apply granular insecticides at planting
Wireworms	leave small hole in tuber. Pest associated with long-term grass	avoid growing potatoes after long-term grass
Cutworms	associated with weedy crops	effective weed control
Slugs	particularly on heavier, or irrigated soils. Some varieties particularly susceptible e.g.Cara	apply slug pellets into growing crop
Colorado Beetle	notify the Ministry of Agriculture if you suspect you have found it	notification scheme has so far prevented establishment in the UK

Disease Control

The potato crop is subject to many diseases of fungal, viral and bacterial origin. Most pose a threat to marketable yield and therefore profitability.

HEALTH

VIRAL

Disease	Significance	Control
Potato Virus X (Mild Mosaic)	up to 15% yield loss symptoms difficult to diagnose. Not aphid transmitted	resistant varieties certified seed aphicide sprays
Potato Virus Y (Severe and Rugose Mosaic)	plants often killed completely. Aphid transmitted	
Leaf Roll Virus	most common viral disease. Up to 50% yield reduction. Aphid transmitted	
Tobacco Rattle Virus (T.R.V.)	transmitted in soil by free living nematodes. Causes spraing symptoms in tubers	
Potato Mop Top Virus (P.M.T.V.)	spread in soil by powdery scab fungus	

FUNGAL

Blight	most significant. Regular routine sprays essential. Secondary phase attacks tubers	resistant varieties; fungicide sprays; early burning off.
Common Scab	variable symptoms. Encouraged by dry seasons and alkaline soils	resistant varieties; irrigation
Powdery Scab	severe infection results in deformed tubers. Encouraged by damp, compacted seedbeds	well prepared seedbeds
Rhizoctonia (Black scurf &Stem Canker)	affected tubers not suitable for pre-packing	fungicidal seed treatments

HEALTH

BACTERIAL

Disease	Significance	Control
Blackleg	decay spreads from lower stems via stolons to tubers, which subsequently rot in store	use certified seed varietal resistance. Avoid planting into cold, wet soils

STORAGE DISEASES

(F - Fungal, B - Bacterial)		
Gangrene (F)	disease enters through site of mechanical damage	avoid mechanical damage during harvest
Dry Rot (F)	affected tubers unmarket-able	careful harvesting. Treat - fungicide
Skin Spot (F)	diseased tubers unsuitable for pre-packing	regulate temp-erature & relative humidity
Silver Scurf (F)	diseased tubers unsuitable for pre-packing	chemical treatment
Soft Rot (B)	tuber phase of blackleg. Adjacent tubers rot.	monitor crop reg-ularly during harvest

There is growing concern over chemical treatment of stored potatoes to control disease or sprouting or both. In future we must concentrate on cultural rather than chemical measures.

LEGAL ASPECTS

F.E.P.A. (Food And Environmental Protection Act)

Covers the application of all pesticides. Intended to safeguard the operator, the eventual consumer and the environment as a whole.

HEALTH

C.O.S.H.H. (Control Of Substances Hazardous To Health)

Essentially, a further clarification of the Health and Safety at Work Act. It is the responsibility of the employer to make an adequate assessment of the risks from hazardous substances, (including pesticides, harmful micro-organisms, dust, etc.) and decide on the control measures to prevent exposure.

NOTIFIABLE PEST

Colorado Beetle

This is a well established potato pest in America and Europe but has failed to establish in the UK The beetle is about 10mm long and broadly oval in shape rather like a large ladybird. Colorado beetles are black and yellow stripped. The beetle and its larvae are leaf eaters and can rapidly strip the haulm.

Any suspected outbreaks must be reported to official organisations, for example the Ministry of Agriculture, Fisheries and Food (M.A.F.F.).

CONTRACTORS CHARGES

Typical Operations

Operation	£/ha
Stone and clod windrowing	172.95*
Planting (2 row/automatic)	50.05*
Haulm chopping	29.65
Harvest (2 row/unmanned)	222.40
* These are cheaper as a combined operation	

HEALTH

HARVESTING

HARVESTING AIM

Harvest maximum, leave behind minimum. Small tubers left in the field may become volunteers (unwanted crop plants) in subsequent crops.

Harvest when soils are still warm and dry for in cold conditions tubers are more susceptible to damage. In wet conditions, soil adheres to the crop, introducing storage diseases.

The grower should minimise any mechanical damage to tubers in order to maintain quality.

TIMING

Harvesting should preferably be in early Autumn to fulfil the requirements above, once the optimum yield has been produced - usually late September and throughout October.

Pre-Harvest Treatments

Some varieties/crops may continue to grow late into the season and it is important to stop them to ensure skins are set before harvesting can commence.

Techniques/treatments:

i	by application of sulphuric acid (contractor operation)
ii	apply a dessicant e.g. 'Reglone' (Diquat)
iii	mechanical pulverisation.

Why Stop The Crop Growing?

To ensure that the grower can harvest in reasonable soil temperature and moisture conditions. Stopping the crop also:

- reduces tuber skin disease
- hastens skin-set
- avoids disease (e.g. blight) spreading from foliage to tubers
- avoids premature sprouting in store
- controls tuber size (crops left too long could become over-sized)

HARVESTING

POTATO STORAGE

Potatoes continue to respire, giving off heat, carbon dioxide and water. Water loss in particular reduces tuber quality. Minimise respiration therefore by controlling temperature and relative humidity, ideally in an environmentally controlled store. Such stores enable long term storage throughout April/May.

In addition storage must aim to control disease and sprouting.

Key Stages

1 **Loading into store** - install ventilation ducts, remove loose soil, grade to remove stones, diseased tubers, etc., avoid mechanical damage.

2 **Apply any necessary storage chemicals** to control sprouting and fungus (N.B. in view of growing public opposition to chemical treatments, the use of such products may reduce marketing opportunities in future). Technazene (sprout suppressant) Maximum Residue Level (M.R.L.) of 5ppm have recently been set.

3 **Crop conditioning:**

i cover with straw to prevent greening, assist insulation and absorb condensation

ii curing period - allow temperatures to remain at 10 - 15 °C for 2 to 3 weeks to assist the healing of wounds

iii ventilate, potatoes must be kept dry in store

iv regulate storage temperatures, according to intended market

Market	Optimum temperature (°C)
ware market, long term	4 - 5
ware market, short term	5 - 8
processing market e.g. crisps and chips	8 - 10
seed, to prevent sprouting	2 - 4

vi sprout control - by maintaining temperatures below 4°C (not applicable for processing crops. See note) and by chemical treatment

vii store unloaded - allow temperatures to rise again to 7 to 12°C to reduce susceptibility to damage from handling

HARVESTING

Note: Low temperature potato storage i.e. below 8°C increases the tubers reducing sugar content, leading to a dark discolouration when processing into crisps or chips.

Such low temperature sweetening can at least be partially reversed by a brief period of higher temperature, usually 15°C - 20°C for 2 to 3 weeks at the end of storage.

CROP RESIDUE DISPOSAL

Excessive potato haulm can be collected and burnt. Leave any discarded potatoes on the soil surface where hopefully they will be killed by subsequent frost rather than produce volunteers.

HARVESTING EQUIPMENT AND COSTS

Options:

i   hand picking, following an elevator digger

ii   a trailed, manned harvester 1 or 2 rows

iii a trailed, unmanned 2 row harvester. (On most soils stone and clod separation would be essential before such machines could be used)

Potato machinery costs	(£)		
2 - 4 row haulm pulveriser	3500	-	8000
2 row elevator digger	3000	-	10000
1 row manned harvester	9000	-	30000
2 row manned harvester	26500	-	45000
2 row unmanned harvester	20000	-	32500
stone and clod separator	9500	-	26000
Potato contracting operation	**£/ha**		
haulm chopping	29.65		
haulm dessication - acid	64.25		
harvesting - digger (2 row)	172.95		
2 row unmanned	222.40		

Source: A.B.C.

HARVESTING

STORAGE COSTS

Options

Bulk	vs	Box storage
building can be used for other purposes		boxes expensive to buy and maintain
max storage depth 3.5 m		allows greater segregation
deterioration e.g. rotting quickly spreads		improved quality control

	£ Per tonne stored
box store with re-circulation fans	102
pallet boxes, 1 tonne	37
bulk store, building only	110
ventilation system and ducts etc.	23

Source: J Nix

OUTSIDER'S GUIDE

KEY ASSESSMENT QUESTIONS

Output varies according to:

YIELD (t/ha)	x	PRICE £/t =	OUTPUT
variety		variety e.g. King Edwards, Maris Piper, Cara etc. attract premium prices	
soil type and season			
availability of irrigation		quality e.g. skin finish	
level of inputs e.g. fertiliser and pesticide		chosen market level of contracted price	
overall husbandry/production skills		time of marketing seasonal affects upon supply & demand level of imports	

NOTES:

Earlies - Average yield, approximately 20 tonnes/hectare. Price varies with the time of lifting and is inversely related to yield. For example, lift early, low yield but high price.

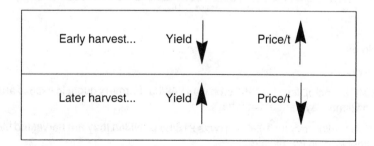

Inputs - Very similar for all producers, whether final yield is high or low. Although there may be slight differences in the amount spent on herbicides and fungicides etc. between high and low yielders, the main influence is the management skill applied and other environmental factors.

PERFORMANCE

GROSS MARGIN ANALYSIS

		Maincrop	Earlies
Production level t/ha		40	20
Price/tonne		70	125
Output		**2800**	**2500**
Variable costs			
Seed	2.8t @ £140/t	392	
	3.6t @ £180/t		648
Fertiliser	220N:250P:275K kg	192	
	180N:250P:135K kg		159
Sprays:		285	140
Casual labour	40 hours harvester	560	
	25 hours harvester		280
P.M.B. ordinary levy		48	12
Sacks at £5/tonne		240	120
Total variable costs		**1717**	**1359**
GROSS MARGIN/ha		**1083**	**1041**

Source: A.B.C.

Notes

Levy

PMB Maincrop levy for 1993 crop was £48/ha. Farmers quota in excess are to incur an additional payment of £480/ha.

PMB Earlies levy for 1994 crop was £12/ha provided they are harvested by 30th June. Otherwise as for maincrop.

(The PMB is to end by 1996).

MAINCROP - G.M. SENSITIVITY ANALYSIS

Assuming : constant variable costs of £525/ha (fertiliser, chemicals and P.M.B. levy)

seed, charged at double the selling price

constant seed rate of 3t/ha

sacks at £6.10/t and casual labour at £14/t (both related to yield).

		Yield in tonnes/ha						
		28	31	34	37	40	43	46	49
Price	**50**	35	125	215	305	395	485	575	665
£/per	**55**	147	252	357	462	567	672	777	882
tonne	**60**	259	379	499	619	739	859	979	1099
	65	371	506	641	776	911	1046	1181	1316
	70	483	633	783	933	1083	1233	1383	1533
	75	595	760	925	1090	1255	1420	1585	1750
	80	707	887	1067	1247	1427	1607	1787	1967
	85	819	1014	1209	1404	1599	1794	1989	2184

Source: A.B.C.

MARKET 1992/93

Pre pack quality samples for the super-market trade continue to attract premium prices of upto £50/tonne. Even tuber size and very good skin finish are essential attributes.

Imports from Europe especially Holland, France and Belgium remain a threat especially following increased plantings blamed on the uncertain outlook for oilseeds and cereals.

TYPICAL FIXED COSTS

Profitable farms manage to minimise fixed costs, and to maximise output from their type of farming system so that fixed costs per unit output are as low as possible.

The figures below are typical levels of fixed costs for an intensive arable farm with at least 5% in roots and/or vegetables. Individual farms will vary in their levels of fixed costs for specific reasons - e.g. new farms will have high **rental charges of 40% to 70%** higher than those quoted. **Larger farms** will tend to have lower costs/hectare.

PERFORMANCE

Intensive Arable Farm of 100 - 200 ha	
(> 5% land for root / vegetable crops)	
FIXED COSTS:	**£ / HECTARE**
Regular labour	240
Depreciation	140
Repairs, tax and insurance - equipment	65
Fuel and electricity	45
Contract charges - hedging/ditching	30
Land maintenance (fencing, repairs etc).	25
Rent & rates	140
Fees, office expenses	65
TOTAL	**750**

Source: A.B.C.

Average Tenant's Capital

This is the value of investment normally provided by the tenant such as machinery, crops in store and other assets required to run the business.

Intensive Arable Farm ≥ 100 hectares	£/ha
Livestock	100
Crops and cultivations	475
Machinery & equipment	725
TOTAL	**1300**

Source: A.B.C.

THE
OUTSIDER'S GUIDE
to
SUGAR BEET

1995 Edition

Outsiders Guide

THE
OUTSIDER'S GUIDE
to
SUGARBEET

1991 Edition

WORLD SITUATION

There is currently a shortage of sugar throughout the world. Stocks are at their lowest for almost ten years at 27% of consumption compared to 43% at the last period of high world prices in 1983/84. However, world prices are notoriously volatile, doubling or halving within a few months.

Consumption is growing slowly at 1 percent a year due largely to alternative sweeteners now on the market. Within this world production, white sugar from beet now accounts for an increasing proportion. This is because beet growers are able to respond faster to changes in demand than are cane producers due to a shorter production cycle.

With the opening up of the Eastern European nations, it is expected that production will increase by 20% over the next five years. This extra production may well be at the expense of cane sugar producers in the third world. (Source Agra Europe Outlook Conference)

PRODUCTION IN THE EU

National Quota System

Production of white sugar from Sugar Beet is regulated by a National Quota System within the EU. Each member country is allocated an 'A' Quota in terms of tonnes of white sugar. In the UK this is about 1/2 of our needs, most of the remaining sugar being produced from sugar cane imported under agreements with the Commonwealth Sugar Producing Countries.

In addition a 'B' Quota is also allocated, this being expressed as a percentage of the 'A' Quota. The UK 'B' Quota is 10%. In other member countries such as France the 'A' & 'B' Quota is double its national consumption. Only UK and Portugal grow less than their consumption. 'C' Quota is any sugar surplus to 'A' & 'B' Quota, it is sold on the world market.

UK Imports

The quantity of sugar imported into the UK balances production from sugar beet. The imported cane sugar comes from commonwealth countries.

Trends

Currently EU sugar quota is about 13.7m tonnes. Consumption is only 11.9m tonnes. The EU is negotiating the sugar regime in relation to the GATT commitments.

PRODUCTION

PRODUCTION IN UK

Historically sugar beet was processed into white sugar by 13 separate companies. In the 1930's an Act of Parliament amalgamated home grown sugar and the British Sugar Corporation was formed to manage the British Crop.

The government sold its share in B.S.C. in 1981 and in January 1991 British Sugar PLC. was taken over by Associated British Foods (A.B.F.). Beet sugar products are probably better known as Silver Spoon.

Today

Over half of Britains' sugar requirement is produced from home grown sugar beet.

In the UK Sugar Beet is grown under contract with British Sugar and processed in their 9 sugar factories. Production is concentrated around these factories.

Each factory has an agricultural manager whose basic job is to make sure that the growers turn up with the beet. These factory managers have staff who liaise closely with the growers and are the growers' first line of contact with the factory.

Beet Sugar Production In The UK

9,600 growers grow 195,000 hectares of sugar beet. These 195,000 hectares yield about 8,000,000 tonnes of sugar beet.

These 8,000,000 tonnes of sugar beet are delivered to the 10 sugar factories between October and the end of January and processed into 1,144m tonnes of 'A' & 'B' Quota sugar plus 350,000 tonnes of cane sugar.

PRODUCTION

WHY GROW THE CROP?

☛ A good cash crop, Sugar Beet is one of the few crops which has a Guaranteed Price.

An average crop of 40t/ha is worth £1680/ha.

☛ It provides a break from cereal crops.

☛ It provides a valuable by-product on the farm for winter feed i.e. Sugar Beet tops, animal feed.

☛ It provides other valuable animal feed by-products in the form of Molassed Sugar Beet Pulp, the residue of the beet after the sugar has been extracted and molasses.

KEY ASSESSMENT QUESTIONS

Production level t/ha	42.5
Price/tonne (@ 17% sugar) £	38.00
Output £	1785.00
Variable costs £	615.00
Gross margin/ha £	**1170.00**

PRODUCTION

FACTORS AFFECTING MARGINS

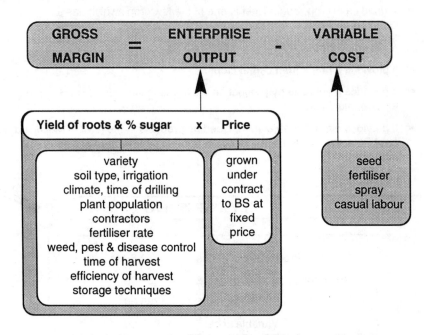

GROSS MARGIN = **ENTERPRISE OUTPUT** - **VARIABLE COST**

Yield of roots & % sugar x Price

variety
soil type, irrigation
climate, time of drilling
plant population
contractors
fertiliser rate
weed, pest & disease control
time of harvest
efficiency of harvest
storage techniques

grown under contract to BS at fixed price

seed
fertiliser
spray
casual labour

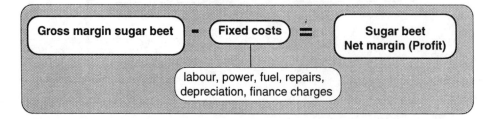

Gross margin sugar beet - **Fixed costs** = **Sugar beet Net margin (Profit)**

labour, power, fuel, repairs, depreciation, finance charges

THE PRODUCTION CYCLE - SUGAR BEET

SEPTEMBER	**PERENNIAL WEED CONTROL / SUB-SOILING**
OCTOBER	
NOVEMBER	Apply fertilizer (non-N) & Plough
DECEMBER	
JANUARY	Machinery maintenance
FEBRUARY	
MARCH	**MINIMUM CULTIVATE & DRILL**
APRIL	Apply seed-bed fertilizer & check for pest damage
MAY	
JUNE	**APHID & WEED CONTROL** — Refer to British Sugar warnings
JULY	
AUGUST	**MILDEW CONTROL**
SEPTEMBER	Prepare harvesting equipment
OCTOBER	**HARVESTING DELIVERY &/OR CLAMP**
NOVEMBER	
DECEMBER	
JANUARY	**DELIVER LAST BEET**
FEBRUARY	**CLEAN CLAMPS**

PRODUCTION

PRODUCTS

Main product:	Sugar 56% of UK market

By products:

i	Sugar beet tops	grazed in field ensiled (very few) ploughed back into land
ii	Molassed sugar beet	high energy animal feed specially compounded for cattle, sheep, pigs and horses.
iii	Molasses	food and chemical industry.

OUTLETS

The crop is grown entirely under contract with British Sugar for delivery during the Campaign period when the beet is processed. The UK utilises all its home produced sugar. The UK production quotas, as assigned by EU, allow virtually no access to the world market.

PRICE

This is fixed in spring each year.

Price is stated as £/tonne of clean sugar beet at 16% sugar content. Thus proportional adjustments are made for sugar percentages above or below this standard 16%. This adjustment is equal to a ± 0.9% price change for each 0.1% above or below 16%.

Early Deliverance Allowance

This is paid for delivery of beet within the first 10 days of the October Beet Campaign. It helps compensate for reduced yield caused by early harvest. This is so that enough beet is brought in quickly to get processing factories working to full capacity. One off negotiation for the 92-93 crop due to early campaign start date. 18% on minimum beet price per tonne on a decreasing scale of 1% per day for 18 days.

Delivery on October	Bonus% of Minimum Beet Price	Delivery on October	Bonus % of Minimum Beet Price
1	10	6	5
2	9	7	4
3	8	8	3
4	7	9	2
5	6	10	1

MARKETING

Late Delivery Allowance

For the 94-95 crop from 26th Dec to 7th Jan there is an 0.8% increase on the price per tonne and from 8th, there is a 0.2% per day of minimum beet price as long as deliveries of A, B, C quota continue.

Transport Allowance

In addition to the value of beet the grower is also paid a transport allowance. This is worked out on an agreed transport distance between farm and factory. The allowance at the distance of 26 miles will be £4.10/clean tonne

LEVIES

For every tonne of clean beet delivered to the factory the grower pays three levies:

1 A levy to N.F.U. to cover cost of representing growers in negotiation with B.S.C. and cost of staff who ensure growers are properly represented when the value of their beet is assessed.

2 Rhizomania levy S.B.R.E. (Sugar Beet Rhizomania Eradication scheme)- intended to raise funds to compensate growers affected by this notifiable disease.No Rhizomania levy for 1992-93 as there were no outbreaks in the previous year.

1994/95	Levy
N.F.U.	8.5 p/tonne + Vat
S.B.R.E. Levy	11p
N.F.U. Rhizomania	
Compensation Scheme	1.3p

Part of the S.B.R.E. goes to producing the **Sugar Beet Review**, a first class quarterly magazine which helps keep up to date all growers and others associated with the industry.

QUOTAS

The National Quota is converted from tonnes of white sugar to the equivalent weight of sugar beet at 16% sugar and growers contract to produce this.

MARKETING

Contracts

Growers contract to produce a specific tonnage of beet at 16% sugar - mostly 'A' Quota plus 10% which is 'B' Quota. This is called the Combined Quota, and is paid for at a fixed price.

Any beet in excess of this Combined Quota is called 'C' Quota. The farmer is paid a delivery allowance for this but will not receive further payment until its value has been calculated in relation to the open market or world price for sugar.

If a grower fails to meet contractual demands in any two of three consecutive years, his Quota will be reduced.

If averaging the best two years from the last three gives a result which is under quota, then that deficit amount is removed from next years quota, so reducing it to the expected realistic production.

Grower Support

Negotiations with British Sugar are carried out on behalf of the growers by the National Farmers Union.

VARIETIES

Growers now have a number of seed fungicide dressing choices e.g. - Pink: treated seed and Green : Fungicide & Insecticide (Force) or Blue Fungicide & Insecticide (Gaucho) seed treatment to control soil pests (Millipedes etc.) but not docking disorder. Also "Gaucho" seed treatment (Blue Pellet) controls soil pests and gives early aphid control.

1995 List Of Varieties

Fully Recommended 1994	Provisionally Recommended 1994
Celt	Aztec
Giselle	Cordelia
Planet	Druid
Saxon	Fiona
	Roberta
	Rose
	Torc
	Tornado
	Triumph
	Vyper
	Zulu

MARKETING

KEY ASSESSMENT QUESTIONS

Varieties are assessed and compared in terms of:

> **Yield**
> **Quality**
> **Bolting (running to seed)**
> **Size of tops**
> **Disease resistance**
> **Percentage establishment.**
> **Growers' income**
> **Crown height (may affect ease of harvesting).**

LEGAL ASPECTS

A grower contracts to produce sugar beet. The legal aspects and contractual definitions are laid out in the Inter-Professional Agreement, an agreement between British Sugar and the National Farmers Union.

Each year growers receive a letter from British Sugar enclosing the contract to be signed. The covering letter states the price arrangements under the following headings:

> **Uniform price per adjusted beet tonne**
>
> making up the UK quota within the EU It explains how much of the quota is already used up by beet carried forward from the previous season.
>
> **The Fall-back Price**
>
> payable if the total production is less than the quota allocation for this season
>
> **The 'C' Beet**
>
> all sugar produced in excess of the total quota for the new season
>
> **Linear Sliding Scale**
>
> provides the actual price paid if total beet production in tonnes falls between the uniform price production level and the Fall-back price production level.
>
> **Transport Allowance**
>
> is calculated on a formula which is used from year to year. e.g. 1990/91 this was (80p + 9.41p per mile) X 1.15 per tonne of clean beet delivered.

INTRODUCTION

Essentially a sugar beet crop converts sunshine into sugar. The crop's leaves intercept the sunlight and absorb carbon-dioxide essential for the conversion of sunlight to sugar. Other requirements for this conversion are met from the soil. The most important is water.

The ideal environment should provide maximum sunlight and optimum carbon-dioxide and water.

Provision of sunlight and carbon-dioxide are beyond the farmer's control, but he can influence, to some extent, by his choice of correct soils for the crop, the correct management of the soil, and of course by irrigation.

Beet production is concentrated around the 10 factories, 2 in the West Midlands - Kidderminster and Telford and the other 8 in Eastern England between York and Ipswich.

Wind erosion of soil can be a major problem on light and peaty soils.

SOILS

Sands

Advantages	Disadvantages
Easy earlier seedbed prep	Drought prone
Earlier drilling	Acidity often a problem
Easier harvest when going gets tough	May risk erosion by wind Prone to a docking disorder
	(caused by free living mematodes)
Longer growing season	Prone to manganese deficiency

Medium textured soils

Advantage	Disadvantages
Ability top produce seedbeds	May get sticky when harvest time is wet

ENVIRONMENT

Heavier soils

Advantages	Disadvantages
Drought resistant	Easily damaged by compaction
Capable of very high yields	Seed beds difficult when no frost mould occurs over winter
	Harvest often difficult

Organic or peat soils

Advantages	Disadvantages
Easy seed bed prep	High cost of weed control
Root yields very high	Risk of wind erosion
Leaf yields very high	Often acidic
Harvest usually early	Lower percentage sugar

DRAINAGE

Good drainage is essential in all soils where beet is to be grown. Symptoms of bad drainage in previous crops must be recognised and rectified well before the beet crop is sown.

ROTATION

The contract states that

"The Grower shall not in any Contract Year sow sugar beet on any land which in either the later or the earlier of the two immediately preceding Contract Years was sown with either sugar beet or any other members of the Beta species such as fodder beet, mangolds, red beet, etc."

This measure was introduced in 1987 as part of the measures to prevent the outbreak of the disease Rhizomania. Previously a 2 year break between host crops was necessary to prevent beet cyst nematode problems.

Host crops of the nematode include not only Beta species but also most cruciferous crops including rape, kale, cauliflower, swede, turnip and Brussels sprouts.

Beet grown more frequently than once in 3 years in one field gives rise to weed beet problems.

Examples Of Rotations

a) Very intensive rotation where soil quality allows winter cereals to be sown after sugar beet.

Year	
1	Sugar beet
2	Winter cereals
3	Winter cereals

b) Very intensive rotation. Tops of beet grazed by sheep over winter and each followed by spring cereals (often Malting Barley).

Year	
1	Sugar beet (Tops grazed in situ)
2	Spring cereals
3	Cereals

c) Wider rotation where beet helps spread the pressure of work in August and September and early October.

Year	
1	Sugar beet
2	Winter wheat
3	Set-aside
4	OSR
5	Winter wheat
6	Winter wheat

ENVIRONMENT

IRRIGATION

Irrigation can offset the effect of a dry year on those soils not very moisture retentive. This is particularly important in the need to achieve full 'A' and 'B' Quotas.

On sandy soils as well as enhancing growth, irrigation may be used as a fire engine treatment to help reduce soil erosion by wind. Irrigation during June, if necessary, can help sugar beet to develop the deep roots needed to withstand drought later on.

Is Irrigation Going To Be Worthwhile?

This question can only be answered by determining how often it is necessary, and how much water would have to be applied.

This will depend on:

> Soil type
> Local climate

Scheduling the irrigation over the growing period is often determined by using a Soil Water Balance sheet.

+ Credits	- Debits	*Balance
Rainfall Irrigation	Evaporation from soil and Plant Drainage	Soil moisture deficit

* This can never be in Credit since extra water should drain away rapidly on a soil growing sugar beet. The level of Deficit will determine the timing and quantity of irrigation required. As the plant grows and roots go deeper, higher levels of deficit can be withstood.

12 O'clock Wilt Or Temporary Wilt

In late summer it is common for the crop to show signs of wilting during the hottest part of the day. However, it is able to recover when the weather cools down.

There is sufficient water available in the soil but because of the very hot conditions, rate of water loss from the leaves is greater than the rate at which roots can take up water from the soil.

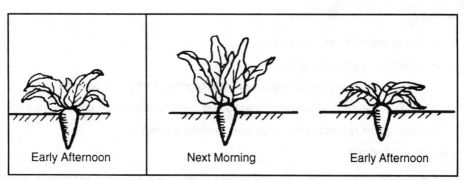

| Early Afternoon | Next Morning | Early Afternoon |

CULTIVATION

The aim should be to produce:

i   a level seedbed in which the sugar beet drill can work efficiently

ii a fine moist tilth at seed depth to give good soil to seed contact for rapid seed germination

iii soil below the seed which is free of compaction through which the roots can penetrate easily to exploit the soils potential, and water can drain easily

Do...

☛ Examine soils for pans or compacted layers and take the necessary action - usually subsoil the previous autumn when soil conditions permit effective cultivation.

☛ Dispose of perennial weeds and previous crop residues without leaving wads of straw under the surface. Chopped straw breaks down quicker. Stubble cultivation helps break down too. Usually reversible ploughs leave surface fairly level.

☛ Leave the soil in a state which will allow it to benefit from the weather before drilling

   heavy soils over winter and frost action should start tilth formation

   lighter soils may be ploughed late and pressed or not ploughed at all where wind erosion is a major risk.

☛ Minimise cultivations for seed bed preparation because extra passes destroy structure, cause compaction, waste fuel, waste time and delay drilling.

ENVIRONMENT

Do Not...

- ☛ Try to subsoil in wet conditions.
- ☛ Plough in great wads of straw.
- ☛ Use seedbed preparation equipment that is going to smear or pan soil.
- ☛ Use seedbed preparation equipment that is going to drag up raw unweathered soil.
- ☛ Attempt the record number of passes to make a seedbed.

Controlled Wheelings

These systems allow cultivation and drilling to take place without risking sowing seed in wheelings. The most obvious way is to drill into ploughed & pressed soil or direct into soil.

These maybe refined further to beds where rows are laid out in groups to match the harvester. Sometimes the gaps between beds are greater than the gaps between rows in the beds in order to prevent damage to the crop by wide tractor tyres.

Wind Erosion

On high risk soil this may result in:

i   Uncovered seed - Leading to poor germination & attack from field mice

ii   Soil & seed blown away completely

iii Chemical treated soil being blown into other susceptible crops.

iv Seedlings cut off or seriously sand blasted.

Anti-Erosion Techniques

i   Chemical bonding agents are very expensive and difficult to apply.

ii   Drilling beet between rows of spring cereals sown about 3 weeks earlier and killed off when beet established with 4 to 6 leaves.

iii Planting straw between every 5 or 6 rows of beet grown on high organic matter soils.

iv Cultivation techniques which keep soil surface tight - plough press and drill without further seed bed preparations.

v   Direct drilling into unploughed soil.

Emergency

When soil is actually blowing away, techniques such as application of slurry, sugar factor lime, broiler muck, or water may help to bind soil surface and stop particles moving.

GROWTH STAGES

THE SUGAR BEET PRODUCTION CYCLE

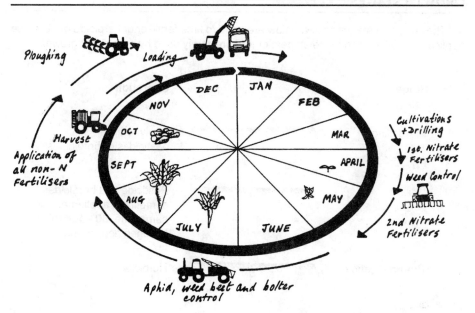

GROWTH STAGES

GROWTH STAGES

The important stages shown below are used to time fertiliser or herbicide or pesticide application. Other than these stages, others are rarely used by sugar beet growers.

Stage		Operation
Pre-drilling		Apply fertiliser, soil pesticides or herbicides
Drilling		Pesticide and herbicides sometimes applied at same time. 30 - 40kg Nitrogen applied after
Pre-emergence		Herbicides
Cotyledon stage		Pesticides and herbicides
Two leaf stage		Remainder of nitrogen and herbicides
Four leaf stage		Crop established

OUTSIDER'S GUIDE

NUTRITION

INTRODUCTION

Fertilisers usually represent the largest variable cost. Their effectiveness is reduced enormously if conditions (such as pH) are not correct. Similarly, too much nitrogen and phosphate with insufficient sodium, frequently depress profits. In an effort to save costs growers must not overlook the nutrient content of Farm Yard Manure or slurry applied.

NUTRIENT REQUIREMENTS

Nutrients should be applied according to what the **crop requires** and what the **soil can provide.**

A good crop removes from the soil approximately:-

65kg	Nitrogen
30kg	Phosphate
90kg	Potash
10kg	Sodium
10kg	Magnesium
60kg	Calcium

Soil Analysis

Soil analysis will determine nutrient status i.e. what the **soil can provide**.

British Sugar offer several soil assessment services.

i   Full soil sample: Sample soil, prepare pH map, provide P:K Mg test results and consultancy advice on fertilisers. Cost £3.00/ha + £7.90/sample.

ii pH sample only: Sample soil, prepare pH map & give advice on use of lime. Cost £3.00/ha.

iii Soil analysis only: You collect the samples, British Sugar test samples and give written report. Cost £7.90/sample.

Similar services are offered by A.D.A.S., fertiliser companies and commercial laboratories.

Note

Care must be taken to ensure that any sample sent for analysis is representative of the whole situation.

NUTRITION

Guidelines For Effective Soil Sampling.

Take one soil sample for each distinct soil type in the field. Each sample should represent no more than 5ha. A sample should be made up of soil taken from 20 - 25 locations from a 'W' pattern walked across the field.

'W' Pattern Sampling

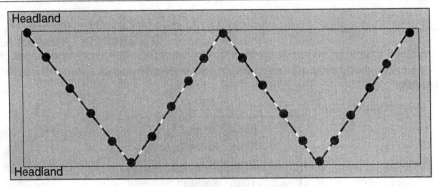

Soil pH

Target pH	6.5 - 7.0	Mineral soils
Target pH	5.8 - 6.5	Peat soils

These pH figures should be achieved by the Autumn before the sugar beet crop is sown. pH above or below these standards influence the uptake of other soil nutrients.

Nitrogen

i   excess nitrogen will make a crop look very green but can have a devastating effect on profitability

ii excess nitrogen increases top growth and as a result the plant has to use much of the energy it has made to feed the extra leaves rather than store this energy in the root where it can be recovered later

iii nitrogen fertiliser close to seeds will cause scorch leading to poor emergence and patchy crops

iv excess nitrogen in the roots also makes the task of recovering the sugar less efficient, due to the increase in impurities

The message from the book of N:

Put on the right amount at the right time.

OUTSIDER'S GUIDE

Nutrient Application Rates

Kg/ha required according to soil type and previous cropping:

Soil Type	Previous Crop		
	Cereals	Beans Peas Potatoes	Long Term Grass
Nitrogen			
Deep Sand or Shallow Chalk Soils	125	100	75
Other Mineral Soils	100	75	50
Deep Organic Soils	75	50	25
Peaty Soils	50	25	0
N;P;K & Mg			
Phosphate	100	75	50M
Potash + 400 kg Salt	200	100	75
Magnesium	165	85M	Nil

TIMING

Nitrogen. 30 - 40kg/ha immediately after drilling. Remainder at about the 2 leaf stage. This will also reduce the chances of nitrates being washed out of the plants root zone in very wet springs. Later applications than this may lower sugars and increase impurities.

NUTRITION

Phosphate, Potash, Sodium And Magnesium

On most, except the very deficient or very sandy soils, these nutrients can be ploughed in during the autumn. This reduces soil structural damage, prevents risk of seed scorch and the need for extra cultivations in the spring to remove wheelings. On very deficient or sandy soils they can be applied before ploughing in January or February or after ploughing using a low ground pressure vehicle.

The quantity of sodium applied should not affect soil structure.

Trace Elements

The most likely to cause deficiencies in sugar beet are Boron and Manganese. If they are known to be a problem then special fertilisers can be used. If symptoms occur unexpectedly, then control is achieved using Borax or Solubor for Boron deficiency, and Manganese Sulphate or Manganese Chelate for manganese deficiency. There is no control for magnesium deficiency in the growing crop.

Common Deficiency Symptoms

Element	Month	Symptoms
Magnesium	June-July	margins of middle leaves turn yellow between main veins. The leaf edges then turn brown and brittle
Manganese	May onwards	leaves take on a speckled yellowing appearance and become stark and upright in growth. The leaf margins also curl in
Boron	July onwards	centre leaves blacken and growing point dies, heartrot. Older leaf stems take on a brown and corky groove. Shoulder of root becomes dry rotted and brown longitudinal stripes appear inside root

LEGAL ASPECTS

C.O.S.H.H. (Control Of Substances Hazardous To Health)

Regulations affect the storage and use of fertilizer to some extent:

Ammonium nitrate (fertilizer)

This is a fire hazard and hence an assessment of risk must be made under the regulations.

Slurry

Any slurry storage presents potential hazards and a variety of provisions are necessary to minimise risks e.g. warning notices, child proof fencing.

NUTRITION

C.O.S.H.H.

These regulations place a duty on farmers to make an assessment of risk for each and every use of materials which could harm users or third parties. The procedure involves the following steps:

1　Identify and list all likely pest problems

2　Assess alternatives to chemical application to check whether it is possible to avoid chemical use

3　Identify alternative chemicals to do the job

4　Check the possible hazards in each case

5　Assess the site of application (is it near habitation, footpath, livestock, inside a building, etc.)

6　Assess method of application

7　Assess necessary precautions and safety equipment

8　Choose the least hazardous alternative chemical method that will fulfil the required purpose

9　Choose appropriate safety equipment

10　Re-check decision process.

(Source: British Agrochemicals Association Ltd. Plain Man's Guide to Pestcides and the COSHH Assessment.)

TYPICAL COSTS

Item	Detail	Cost	Work rate
Fertiliser spreader	12 m pneumatic	£4000-8000	3.5 ha/hour
Fertiliser broadcaster	Spinning disk 12 m	£600-5500	2.5 ha/hour
Item	**Detail**	**Cost**	
Fertiliser			
Straight Nitrogen	34.5% N	£95-110/tonne	
Compound	0:24:24	£98-105/tonne	
Salt	including spreading	£40/tonne	

NUTRITION

THE DRILL

Before drilling the crop, it is essential that the drill be checked over to ensure that it is capable of working properly. If not seed spacings and drilling depths will be erratic giving rise to gappy uneven crops.

The beet drill should be overhauled first , during January or February growers should make use of the drill unit testing service offered at the British Sugar factories.

Drilling The Crop

Time	
January/February	machine maintenance.
March 20 - early April	do not plant too early for there is more risk of bolting and slower, poorer germination giving uneven crops. But too late and there is loss of potential yield
Row widths	46 cm (18 in) to 54 cm (22 in)
Seed spacing	eventual aim will be 75,000 plants/ha on fertile soils or up to 100,000 plants/ha on thin or shallower soil
Seed depth	the seed must be drilled evenly into moist soil at usually 25 - 30 mm, but deeper if soil is at risk from blowing or from field mouse attack.

INTRODUCTION

A wide range of chemicals are used to protect the beet crop from a wide range of pests including insects, weeds, vectors of diseases and diseases themselves. These chemicals grouped together as pesticides are legally controlled in their marketing, storage, use and disposal under the Food and Environmental Protection Act.

Application Techniques

Granular application

This technique is usually reserved for pesticides designed to control soil borne pests.

Band spraying

In this the pesticide, usually a herbicide, is sprayed on a narrow strip over the seed or plant row allowing weed control by cheaper cultivations in between the rows. It could also be used to apply aphicides to plants when the plants only actually cover about 1/3 of the soil surface.

Low volume spraying

This technique is used mostly for applying post-emergence herbicides. It is essential that the herbicide is applied when the weed targets are in the cotyledon to first true leaf stage. Repeated applications allow efficient weed control of weeds which germinate over a length of time.

Overall spraying

This is probably the most common and today sprayers covering 12 m plus at a time are quite common.

WEED PEST AND DISEASE CONTROL

This is a very demanding subject and many growers will rely on the advice offered by British Sugar, chemical company representatives, advisors and other crop consultants. British Sugar's advice is sure to be economically untainted and easily available.

The shotgun approach of applying chemicals to kill every likely problem pest, weed or disease should it appear is **not viable, economically or environmentally.**

Thresholds exist which determine at which level it becomes worthwhile to control certain pests.

Chemicals vary in their suitability for soils or weather at and after application.

HEALTH

Common Weed, Disease And Pest Control Calendar

PEST/DISEASES	DETAIL	CONTROL
Perennial weeds	e.g. Couch	Control in Autumn before growing sugar beet.
Soil pests	e.g. Springtails Symphylids	Control by seed treatment or granule application before or/at drilling .
Annual grass weeds	e.g. Wildoats	Herbicides worked into seedbed pre-drilling.
Annual broadleaf weeds	e.g. Black bindweed, Knotgrass, Fat hen, Orache, Redshank, Mayweed and many more.	a) Pre-emergence herbicides to kill early germinating weeds. b) Post-emergence herbicides, these control weeds germinating over a much wider time span. Low Dose Programme of herbicides normally used depending on weed size.
Insects 	e.g. Aphids which carry Virus Yellows	British Sugar monitor aphid numbers and issue warnings when control is necessary.
Weed beet and bolters	i.e. Beet which have seeded in first year or products of those seeds from previous years.	a) Pull by hand and destroy. b) Apply contact herbicide selectively.
Diseases	e.g. Mildews	Spray approved fungicide when diseases are found early in the growing season.

Weed Control By Cultivation

Inter-row cultivation by steerage hoe is still carried out in at least 60% of crops. It is cheap and good in situations where chemical alternatives do not exist. However it is quite a slow alternative to spraying and in wet seasons often only transplants weeds.

Use of inter-row cultivations requires a very high level of operator efficiency in order to get the best out of the machine without damaging the crop.

Virus Yellows

This viral disease is carried by aphids and an early attack, yellowing the leaves, could reduce yields by 40-50%.

By destroying sites where aphids collect over winter one will limit the introduction of virus carrying aphids. Infected aphids moving in from weed hosts or other crop hosts must be identified and controlled quickly in order to prevent disease spread.

Timing of foliar spraying is vital and British Sugar notifies growers by post when treatment should start.

Rhizomania

This disease could make beet growing uneconomical. It is a virus disease carried by a common soil fungus. Once present in the soil it will not decline and disappear. In England very strict measures are being taken to prevent the disease from becoming endemic.

It is now a **Notifiable Disease** so if suspected:

i   A grower must consult a British Sugar Advisor, an A.D.A.S. Advisor or the M.A.F.F. Plant Health Inspectorate.
ii A grower must not remove any beet or soil from the farm.

Symptoms include:

Foliage	Pale patches in the crop where leaves are narrow upright and have a long stalk.
	Patches where wilting is more prevalent.
	Some leaves may have yellow veins.
Roots	Round and stunted with a very bearded appearance instead of normal long conical shape (Hour glass effect).
	When cut in half vascular system of root is stained brown.

HEALTH

As part of an ongoing campaign against the spread of Rhizomania,

British Sugar:

i   have cancelled National Beet Harvesting and Spring Demonstrations.

ii   have built wheel baths to allow for disinfection of all vehicles leaving their factories.

ii   examine root samples for signs of disease.

iv   carry out rigorous checks if the sugar % of a sample is 3% or more below the factory average.

v   have stopped soil washes from roots being returned to farm land.

vi   give advice to outside bodies running demonstartions on Rhizomania code of practice.

CROP HYGIENE

As in everything - 'Prevention is better than cure'.

Applied to sugar beet growing this includes:

i   Maintain a healthy rotation - see contract

ii   Destroy old clamp sites as these act as sources of infection for diseases and pests e.g. aphids +virus yellows

iii   Do not allow bolting sugar beet to shed seed as these will grow as weed beet in future crops

iv   Stubble cultivation the previous Autumn helps dispose of many weed seeds

v   Pre-empt problems by knowledge of problems. e.g. Leatherjackets damaging young roots in crop following grass

vi   Ensure that only clean equipment comes onto your farm

vii   Pressure wash machinery and vehicles before leaving the farm and disinfect soil containing parts with a 2% formal dehyde solution to kill the fungus carrying virus.

LEGAL ASPECTS

The major points of importance to beet growers are:

1   Pesticides should be stored in suitable and safe buildings.

2   Empty containers must be disposed of safely.

HEALTH

3 Certification of Competence, workers should be certified or be working under the supervision of a certificated operator. Certification of competence is required by contractors applying pesticide to land not owned by them and people born after December 31st, 1964 not working under the direct supervision of a certificate holder.

4 Pesticide users must only apply chemicals in the manner approved and stated on the label of the pesticide container.

Essential points to remember when applying pesticides:

1 Read and follow instructions on product labels

2 Use protective clothing specified on product label

3 Check that application machinery is in good working order

4 Check that application equipment is properly calibrated

5 Check that climatic conditions are correct

6 Dispose of unapplied chemicals safely

7 Dispose of empty containers safely

8 Clean application equipment after use.

Further details can be obtained in the following publications: The UK Pesticide Guide (1989) British Crop Protection Council. Guide to the New Pesticide Regulations, British Agrochemical Association.

CONTRACTORS & EQUIPMENT CHARGES

Item	Detail	Cost £	Work Rate ha/day
Contracting			
Bolter cutting	-	7.80/ha	-
Bolter spraying	-	6.80/ha	-
Standard Spraying	225l/ha	9.90/ha	-
Equipment			
Sprayers	Mounted 600 - 800 l (12 m)	1500 - 10,000	20

HEALTH

HARVESTING

To lift maximum quantity of correctly topped, undamaged clean sugar beet at maximum sugar percentage.

Correct Topping

Aim for a top tare between 3% and 5%.

If beet is delivered to the factory too dirty, then after a warning it is likely to be returned. Total tare i.e. tops, soil, rubbish, stones should not exceed 15%.

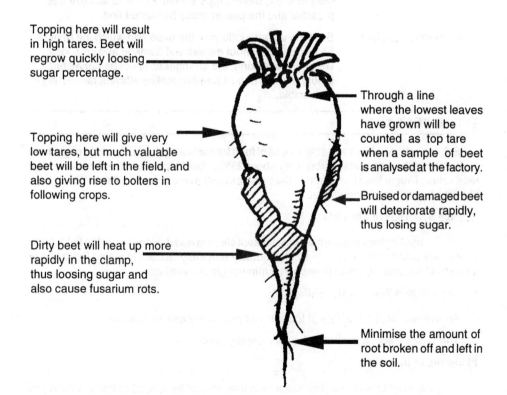

Topping here will result in high tares. Beet will regrow quickly loosing sugar percentage.

Topping here will give very low tares, but much valuable beet will be left in the field, and also giving rise to bolters in following crops.

Dirty beet will heat up more rapidly in the clamp, thus loosing sugar and also cause fusarium rots.

Through a line where the lowest leaves have grown will be counted as top tare when a sample of beet is analysed at the factory.

Bruised or damaged beet will deteriorate rapidly, thus losing sugar.

Minimise the amount of root broken off and left in the soil.

HARVESTING

 Timing

Beet grows throughout the autumn and early winter. As the winter progresses the beet draws on its sugar reserves more and more until sugar yield falls.

1	Mid-November	Maximum yield of sugar is achieved, but of course soil conditions for harvesting could be worsening before then.
2	Early December	The risk of frost increases , therefore, on all but very light soils, beet should be harvested and clamped.
3	Poor crops first	Good crops have a lot better potential than poor crops, therefore, the better crops should be left to achieve this potential and the poorer crops harvested first.
4	Strong soils first	Soil type will also influence the ease with which the beet can be harvested without excess soil damage and crop loss. Generally speaking, the stronger soils will be harvested before the risk of bad weather makes efficient harvesting impossible.

SUGAR BEET TOPS

Sugar beet tops offer a valuable source of food for cattle and sheep, but since sugar beet tends to be grown on arable farms, only about 25% of beet tops are utilised this way. The feed value of sugar beet tops is about the same as fairly average hay or silage. 'Fresh' tops should be wilted for 48 hours first.

Grazing Beet Tops In The Field

For feeding tops ensure that tops are kept clean, avoid driving all over the field. Allow tops to wilt and introduce tops to stock gradually with easy access to water. Feed hay or straw to stock also with high phosphorus mineral blocks available.

Carting-Off Beet Tops To Make Silage

An average of about 24t/ha of tops should produce about 14.5t silage.

The silage made is normally of a very low dry matter.

Ploughing In Beet Tops

If tops are not to be utilised by stock then they should be spread before ploughing in. Some harvesters spread tops quite well, if this is not the case then tops can be spread by cultivators angled to the rows of tops, prior to ploughing. If tops are not spread evenly then following crops often show bands of uneven growth where the tops have been left.

HARVESTING

Storing Beet

Always site in dry accessible positions. Long low clamps, no more than 3 m high, are best for long term storage with a frost cover to hand for use if necessary. Ideal clamp temperature is 0-5°C.

For good quality, only healthy, correctly topped, undamaged beet should be stored with no excess soil, loose tops and other rubbish. Clean clamp site after use and destroy any remaining beet and beet tops.

TRANSPORT

Loading Beet And Transporting

Minimise damage by unloading clamp from the bottom using a cleaner-loader to remove soil and stones if beet is dirty. Return soil from loader sites to the original beet fields and destroy any remaining small beet which have fallen through cleaner.

Growers will be notified of any local factory regulations relating to beet delivery vehicles e.g. minimum weights accepted. All vehicles must have marks indicating position of check chains and internal height of transports floor. This will avoid damage by core samplers.

LEGAL ASPECTS

The normal laws of the road apply to vehicles transporting sugar beet. i.e. Maximum weights for vehicles; Loose and unsafe loads; Maximum transport distance for farm vehicles using 'pink' diesel; Trailers lights, number boards and braking systems and soil and trash left on the roads.

HARVESTING MACHINERY COSTS

Item	Detail	Cost £'000	Work rate ha/day
harvesters	6 row self-propelled	85 - 195	5.0
harvesters	3 row tractor mounted	12 - 40	2.5
harvesters	1 row tractor mounted	12 - 18	0.8
Cleaner loader	-	3 - 15	
6 row 3 stage	topper	7 - 11	
	lifter	7 - 13	
	collector/loader	12 - 20	
Trailer	10 tonne dump	6	
Trailer	14 tonne	10.5	
Contract harvesting		£135/ha	
Transport	20 miles	£4.50/tonne	

HARVESTING

OUTSIDER'S GUIDE

TYPICAL GROSS MARGIN

Output	40t/ha, 16.0% sugar @ £40/t	£1600.00
	(includes transport allowance)	
Variable costs		
Seed	6kg @ £13.00/kg	81
Fertiliser	125N 60P 190K/kg	93
Sprays £	weeds	95
	pests & disease	85
Transport	£4.75/washed tonne	190
Sundries including levies		15
Total variable costs		**£559**
Gross margin/ha		**£1041**

Source: A.B.C.

Output Target

Maximise sugar yield per ha.

In good year 8t sugar per ha is a realistic performance, but average is just over 6.5t.

Variable Costs

Seed (this cost is not highly variable). Fertiliser, herbicides, pesticides, fungicides (these costs are very variable and as individual components can have a big influence on crop yield).

TYPICAL FIXED COSTS

Profitable farms manage to minimize fixed costs, and to maximise output from their type of farming system so that fixed costs per unit output are as low as possible. Many growers have attempted to reduce these by machinery sharing syndicates or by using contractors services, particularly for harvesting.

The figures below are typical levels of fixed costs for an intensive arable farm with at least 5% in roots and/or vegetables. Individual farms will vary in their levels of fixed costs for specific reasons - e.g. new farms will have high RENTAL charges of 40% to 70% higher than those quoted. Larger farms will tend to have lower costs/hectare.

PERFORMANCE

Examples of fixed costs £/ha for Farm of about 200 ha		
Cropping	Beet & combinable crops	Beet, potatoes & combinable crops
	(Mainly cereals)	(Mixed cropping)
Regular labour	160	220
Depreciation	95	125
Repairs, tax, insurance	50	60
Fuel, electricity	32	45
Other contact expenses	20	15
Rent	120	135
Estate maintenance	20	20
Sundries	40	50
Total	**£537**	**£670**

Source: A.B.C.

Average Tenant's Capital

This is the value of investment normally provided by the tenant such as machinery, crops in store and other assets required to run the business.

Mainly cereals farm up to 200ha	£/ha
Livestock	225
Crops and cultivations	390
Machinery & equipment	575
TOTAL	**1190**

Source: A.B.C.

THE
OUTSIDER'S GUIDE
to
CROP PRODUCTION
APPENDIX

1995 Edition

THE
OUTSIDER'S GUIDE
to
CROP PRODUCTION
APPENDIX

1995 Edition

SUPPORT

Support from the European Union currently takes several forms.

These are:

A. IACS & Set Aside	Designed to reduce the surplus of certain products on the European market. This helps maintain market prices through supply control and consequently this reduces the need for intervention buying and storage.
B. Grants	These are available for a number of desirable farm developments. These may be of an environmental nature (trees, alternative land uses) or business development nature helping a marginal farm to become fully
C. Price / product support	Certain products still attract special payments often based on the area grown. self-supporting and to provide more rural employment.

This section on support tells you about the various measures of EU support provided for each of the arable crops summarised in this Outsiders Guide. Common suuport in the form of set-aside or grants are explained first. Specific crop-related support is explained afterwards in the same sequence as the crops appear in the Outsiders Guide i.e. Spring Cereals; Winter Cereals; Linseed; Oilseed Rape; Peas and Beans; Maincrop Potatoes; Sugar Beet.

A. GENERAL FARM SUPPORT

Integrated Administrative & Control System (I.A.C.S)

Anti fraud measure to stop fraudulent claims for grants. I.A.C.S applies to Arable Area Payments, Beef Special Premium and Suckler Cow Premium. The system involves a form filling exercise which includes the submission of O.S. maps to M.A.F.F for identification purposes.

Other parts of the system will comprise of an identification system for each field, a system for identification and registration of certain animals. Penalties for late and inaccurate applications are severe.

SUPPORT

Set Aside

A new set-aside scheme started as from the Autumn 1992 drilling. The payment for land set-aside was £253/ha in 1993, rising to £315/ha in 94/95. The amount of land to be 15% (18% on non rotational set-aside or flexible set-aside) of the land on which area payment can be claimed ie land used for wheat, barley, oats, rye, maize, oilseed rape, peas, field beans and linseed.

Main Features

To compensate for a phased reduction in arable support prices, an area payments scheme has been introduced, paid directly to growers. To qualify for these area payments, growers must set-aside 15% or 18% of their eligible land on which compensation will be paid.

Regional base area ceilings have also been introduced. If compensation claims exceed the regional base area, area payments for all growers in the region will be reduced proportionately, and growers must set-aside additional land the next year. In this way it is hoped to stabilise the EU farm budget.

Land is not eligible if under permanent pasture (more than 5 years), woodland, non-agricultural use, S.S.I., nitrate sensitive area's etc. on 31st December 1991.

Rates Of Payment

These differ according to expected yield potential in differing areas of the UK e.g. in England for example where yields are expected to be greater due to a more favourable climate and better soil types, the level the level of compensation/ha is greater. UK is divided in 7 areas, England, Scotland, Wales and N.Ireland (LFA and non-LFA).

Regional Payment Rates 1994 - 96		
	1994/5	**1995/6**
Cereals	193.53	248.83
Oilseeds	436.88	
Proteins	385.45	
Linseed	481.06	
Set-aside	315.18	315.18
Additional Set-aside	219.69	219.69

NOTE: In the 1994/95 season only there may be a 3% reduction in set-aside requirements.

OUTSIDER'S GUIDE

SUPPORT

B. GRANTS

Environmentally Sensitive Areas (ESAs)

Introduced in 1987 with the aim of conserving the British countryside. 44 areas have been designated ESAs covering 15% of agricultural land. Farmers volunteering are offered a ten year agreement. Annual payments vary between ESA's depending on amount of restrictions on farming activities. Payments of upto £400/ha may be paid.

Countryside Stewardship Scheme

A pilot scheme from the Countryside Commission available in England only, with only 7 target land types eligible including - heath, chalk/limestone grassland, waterside land, coastal areas and upland each contract is for a ten year contract. Payments from £20 to £250/ha plus £50/ha where public access is allowed.

Group Marketing Grant Scheme

This MAFF administered grant is to encourage the formation of new producer groups, and the improvement of existing groups. Scheme contributes 50% of the key management expenses in starting a group - feasibility studies, salaries, legal and training costs. In addition grants of 40 - 30 and 20% are available for the marketing cost for the first 3 years.

Farm And Conservation Grant Scheme

Grants are made available under three main headings; land improvement and energy saving, waste handling facilities, environment and countryside.

Higher rates of grant (50%) generally apply in Less Favoured Areas (LFA's) and also where an improvement plan is submitted. Young farmers under the age of 40 may qualify for an additional 25% above standard rates.

Hedgerow Incentive Scheme

A voluntary scheme designed to both improve existing hedgerows and encourage new ones. Administered by the Countryside Commission. Agreements for 10 years and over for the whole farm.

Grant rates e.g. Gapping up £1.75/metre planted. Hedge laying £2/metre.

SUPPORT

Countryside Access Scheme

Launched in September 1994 for set-aside land which is suited to new or unused public access will be eligible. £90/ha per 10m width access stops along or across fields. Larger areas will pay £45/ha. Land must be managed according set-aside rules.

Organic Aid Scheme

Started on 1st August 1994. Payments will be made for converting to organic farming over 5 years. Approval of the UK Organic Organisation is needed. Starts at £70/ha reducing to £25/ha at end.LFA's will receive only 20 % of grant.

Farm Woodland Premium Scheme

From April 1992 and replaces Farm woodland scheme which ended March 1992. Annual payments of up to £250/ha for planting on arable or improved grassland in Less Favoured Areas (LFAs) for 10 to 15 years according to woodland type. Payments of £60/ha for unimproved grassland in LFAs.

SPECIFIC CROPS SUPPORT

i. Spring & Winter Cereals

ii. Linseed

iii. Oilseed Rape

iv. Peas and Beans

v. Maincrop Potatoes

vi. Sugar Beet.

SUPPORT

I. SPRING & WINTER CEREALS

Intervention Price For 1994-95, Wheat, Barley, Rye

November	1994	102.04
May	1995	108.85

Note: Feed Wheat can no longer be offered for intervention

Minimum Quality Requirement For Intervention

	Common (breadmaking wheat)	Barley
Max. Moisture Content	14.5%	14.5%
Minimum specific weight	72 kg/hl	62 kg/hl
Total impurities	12%	12%
Hagberg Falling No	220	
Zeleny Index	20	
Machinability test	Pass	

Notes: Bonus of 0.1% for each 0.1% the moisture content is below 13.5%. (Max bonus 3.5%)

Reductions for low specific weights down to the minimum of 72 and 62 for wheat and barley respectively. e.g. wheat 74-73 kg/hl 1.5% deduction.

Reductions for low protein contents, but no minimum imposed.

If the Zeleny index is above 30, the sample does not have to pass the machinability test.

II. LINSEED

Linseed is now supported by the arable aid payment scheme and there is a set-aside requirement. In the past there was a seperate scheme co-ordinated by the intervention board. Aid payment vary according to avereage world price and yields. The subsidy for 1994 was £481.06 (1993 £478.16).

Crops must be sown by 15 May to obtain the subsidy. Aid normally paid between 16 October and 31 December of the harvest year.

Flax is excluded from the arable aid scheme. It has its own support scheme currently worth 634.75ECU/ha.

III. OIL SEED RAPE

IACS area aid application must be made by 15 May. If growing oilseed on contract for non-food on set-aside land a delivery declaration must be submitted after harvest.

Land & Variety Implications

For the 93 harvest all plantings must be on land that was in arable crops in the years 89/90, 90/91 and 91/92.

All varieties must be double zero types or those intended for industrial or seed use. The arable land rule will also apply to spring crops sown in 1994.

Seed

Home saved seed is eligible for use but the following rules apply:-

1   Only approved certified rapeseed varieties allowed.

2   All invoices and seed labels must be kept for inspection.

3   Seed intended for home use must have been sampled by an appointed agent of the relevant Agricultural department and an analysis shown to have a glucosinolate content of 18 micromoles per gramme or less. This could stimulate interest in the very low glucosinolate varieties).

4   Seed must have been produced on the holding on which it is to be sown.

5   Seed must be produced, stored and prepared according to good agricultural practice.

6   Must be the crop of that year's harvest, or, in the case of Spring sown rape, of the previous year's harvest.

Rate Of Aid

The aid formula is based on a relationship of 2.1:1 between oilseed rape and cereals. World market prices for cereals and oilseeds are then used to calculate a deficiency payment per tonne in ECU's. This is then multiplied by the EU average yield of 2.36t/ha to produce the oilseeds reference aid in EU's/ha. The level of aid is regionalised throughout the EU and UK according to yield.

UK OILSEEDS REGIONAL AREA PAYMENTS		
REGION	Av. Yield	Aid
ENGLAND	3.08 t/ha	£437
WALES	3.14	£445
N. IRELAND	2.92	£414
SCOT (LFA)	2.84	£404
SCOTLAND	3.45	£489

* Actual will depend on the green rate, plus 2 other factors

1   UK exceeds base area. '94 crop is above the base area of 327,000ha

2   If world price is different (± 8%) from the projected price.

Maximum Guaranteed Area (MGA)

For 94 the final regional reference amount will be reduced by 1% for every 1% of crop grown over the MGA of 3.371million ha for the EU Estimates so far suggest the MGA will not be exceeded and therefore there will be cuts in the regional reference amount.

IV. PEAS & BEANS

The EU Support System

To keep EU budgets in check, a maximum guaranteed quantity (MGQ) of 3.5m tonnes of peas and beans was permitted. For every 1% over-production, the minimum guaranteed price was reduced by 0.5%.

Starting with the 1993 harvest, the support system has been radically altered in response to pressures from GATT (General Agreement on Tariffs and Trade). Pea and bean prices will be allowed to fall to world market levels, but to protect producers incomes, they will be given a hectareage payment of 385ECU/ha. In return, growers must set-aside 15% -18% of their combinable crop area.

The Processors and Growers Research Organisation (P.G.R.O.) carry out important research and development work into peas and beans, and charge a levy of 32 pence per tonne of crop sold.

There is no price support system for **vining peas**. Each year prices are negotiated

SUPPORT

between processors and growers. All vining peas are grown on contract, which means that levels of production can be closely linked to demand.

Most dried peas grown for human consumption are grown on contract, which usually guarantees a substantial premium over feed pea prices.

When growing peas on contract, extreme care should be taken when choosing crop protection chemicals, as the use of certain common chemicals nullifies the agreement.

Higher rates of grant (50%) generally apply in Less Favoured Areas (L.F.A.'s) and also where an improvement plan is submitted. Young farmers under the age of 40 may qualify for an additional 25% above standard rates.

V. POTATOES

2 options available

Pre-season contracts

These are set at prices varying from £47 to £100/t. Mainly for processing markets.

PMB direct intervention scheme

If prices fall below a pre-determined direct intervention trigger price, the PMB buys up the surpluses and disposes of them as livestock feed. Once the immediate surplus is removed, prices then rise above the trigger level.

VI. SUGAR BEET

Price

The UK sugar beet grower is supported by the Common Agricultural Policy structure of internal support, minimum import prices and export refunds.

The price is fixed in spring each year and is stated as £/tonne of clean sugar beet at 16% sugar content. A proportional increase and proportional decrease is made for sugar content above and below the 16%, respectively.

An early delivery allowance is paid for delivery of beet within the first 10 days of the Beet Campaign in October is negotiated by the NFU and British Sugar.

A late delivery bonus is paid to help offset the extra cost incurred in storing beet over winter. A transport allowance is paid per tonne of clean beet delivered.

GATT Negotiations

The EU is negotiating the sugar regime in relation to the GATT commitments. This would mean a cut in sugar support/sugar beet quota.

OUTSIDER'S GUIDE

CONTACTS & TERMS

USEFUL REFERENCES

A.C.P. Publishers	Crop Chemicals Guide
A.D.A.S.	Crop nutrition requirements Nº 209
Agro Business Consultants	The Agricultural Budgeting & Costing Book
British Agrochemical Association	Plain Man's Guide to the New Pesticide Regulations
	Spraying Within the Law
	Disposal Guidelines
British Crop Protection Council	The UK Pesticide Guide
	Nozzle Selection Handbook
	Pest & Disease Control Handbook
	Pesticide Manual
Brooke Bond Foods Ltd	Dried Peas for Human Consumption
Dalgety	Masterseeds Yearbook
Halley RJ and Soffe RJ (1988)	The Agricultural Notebook, London, Butterworths
Harper F (1983)	The Principles of Arable Crop Production, London, Granada Publishing
Health and Safety Executive Publications	A Guide to the Poisonous Substances in Agriculture Regulations 1984 (Booklet HS (R) 20:)
	Poisoning by Pesticides: First Aid (Advice Card MS (B) 7)
	Protective Clothing Wall Chart
	Storage of Pesticides on Farms and Similar Premises
	Safety Features on Agricultural Crop Sprayers - a Check List
M.A.F.F. (Publications)	Farm Chemical Stores (Leaflet 767)
	Use of Fungicides and Insecticides on Cereals (Booklet 2257)
McClean KA (1980)	Drying and Storing Combinable Crops, Ipswich, The Farming Press Ltd

CONTACTS & TERMS

Ministry of Agriculture Publications	Code of Practice on the Agricultural and Horticultural use of Pesticides
	Containers on farms and holdings. (Booklet 2198)
	Reference Book 500: Pesticides 1988 (and succeeding editions)
	Guidelines for the disposal of unwanted pesticides and containers on farms and holdings. (Booklet 2198)
N.I.A.B.	Revised 1994 Spring Cereals Varieties - leaflet No. 8
	Peas and Beans variety list
Nix - Wye College	Farm Management Pocketbook
Processors and Growers Research	Pea Growing Hand Book Organisation
Schering Agriculture	Working with Pesticides - The regulations and your responsibilities
	Weed Guide
	Cereal Disease Guide
	Cash Crops Disease Guide
	Grain Quality Guide
	Pea and Bean pocket book
Sugar Beet Research & Education	Sugar Beet - A Growers Guide, 4th Edition

USEFUL CONTACTS

Agricultural Training Board (ATB)	Head Office, Stoneleigh Park Pavilion, National Agricultural Centre, Kenilworth, Warwickshire, CV8 2UG (01203 696996)
B.A.S.F. United Kingdom Ltd	Lady Lane, Hadleigh, Ipswich, Suffolk IP7 6BQ. Tel: Hadleigh (01473) 822531
British Agrochemicals Association Ltd	(B.A.A.) 4 Lincoln Court, Lincoln Road, Peterborough, Cambridge PE1 2RP (01733 49225)
British Crop Protection Council	(B.C.P.C.) 20 Bridport Road, Thornton Heath, Croydon CR4 7QC (0181 683 0211)

CONTACTS & TERMS

British Standards Inspection Scheme	(B.A.S.I.S.) Bank Chambers, 2 St.John Street, Ashbourne, Derbyshire DE6 1GH (01335 43945)
British Institute of Agricultural Consultants	Durleigh House, 3 Elm Close, Campton, Shefford, Beds. SG17 5PE
Brooke Bond Foods Ltd	Batchelors Factory Claylands Avenue, Gateford Road, Worksop, Notts S81 7AY Tel: (01909 475522)
Broom's Barn Experimental Station	Higham, Bury St. Edmunds, Suffolk IP28 6NP Tel: (0284 810563)
Ciba-Geigy Agrochemicals	Whittlesford, Cambridge CB2 4QT Tel:Cambridge (01223 833621)
Dalgety Agriculture Ltd	Dalgety House, Works Lane, Setchey, Lynn, Norfolk PE33 0AU Tel: 01553 811031
Farming and Wildlife Advisory Group	The Lodge, Sandy, Bedfordshire SG19 2DL (01767 80551)
Flour Milling & Baking Research Association	Chorleywood, Rickmansworth, Herts WD3 5SH
Food From Britain	417 - 418 Market Towers, New Covent Garden Market, London SW8 5N7 (0171 720 7551).
Health and Safety Executive (H.S.E.)	HM Agricultural Inspectorate, Baynards House, 1 Chepstow Place, London W2 4TF (0181 299 3456)
Home Grown Cereals Authority	Hamlyn House, Highgate, London NI9 5PR, (0171 263 3391)
H.M.S.O. Publications Centre,	PO Box 276, London SW8 5OT. (0171 622 3316)
Intervention Board for Agricultural Produce	Fountain House, 2, Queens Walk, Reading, RG1 7QW
Ministry of Agriculture (M.A.F.F.)	3 Whitehall Place,London SW1A 2HH (0171 233 3000)
National Association of Agricultural Contractors	Huts Corner, Tilford Road, (N.A.A.C. Hindhead, Surrey (01428 735360)

CONTACTS & TERMS

National Farmers Union (N.F.U.)	22 Long Acre, London WC2E 9LY (0171 235 5077)
National Institute of Agricultural Botany	Cereals Branch, Huntingdon Road, Cambridge CB3 0LA (01223 276381)
National Proficiency Test Council	(N.P.T.C) Tenth Street, National Agricultural Centre, Stoneleigh, Warwickshire CV8 2LG (01203 56132)
Processors and Growers Research Organisation	The Research Station, Great North Road, Thornhaugh, Peterborough PE8 6HJ. (01780 782585)
Profarma	Nottingham Road, Stapleford, Nottingham NG9 4TZ (01602 390202)
Rhone Poulenc Crop Protection	Regent House, Hubert Road, Brentwood, Essex CM14 4TZ
Royal Agricultural Society of England	Arable Unit, National Agricultural Centre (NAC), Stoneleigh, Kenilworth, Warwickshire CV8 2LZ (01203 555100)
Seed Crushing and Oil Processing Industry	16 Katherine Street, London, WC28 5JJ

TERMS AND ABBREVIATIONS

1st earlies	particularly early maturing varieties, grown in 'early areas' e.g. Devon and Cornwall
2nd earlies	later than 1st earlies, but earlier than maincrops. Grown primarily in the northern and eastern counties
Admixture	non-oilseed rape found in rape samples
Amino Nitrogen	nitrogen in the roots of beet excess of which reduces efficiency of sugar extraction at the factory. Growers should aim to keep amino nitrogen figures as shown on beet return below 150 by correct use of nitrogen fertilizers
Beet Quota	the tonnage of clean beet at 16% sugar which a farmer contracts to produce at fixed price

CONTACTS & TERMS

Beet Sample	a sample, usually about 12kg, which is taken from a random position in a load in order to determine total tare, sugar percentage (and sometimes amino nitrogen) of that load for valuation purposes
Beet Return	a weekly return made by British Sugar which details the assessment and value of the previous weeks deliveries of sugar beet
Biennial	a plant which completes its life cycle over two years, flowering and producing seed in the second year
Bolter	sugar beet which breaks its normal 2 year cycle to flower and seed in its first year
Break crop	a non-cereal crop grown to act as a break to continuous growing of certain crops (eg. between two cereals)
Calibration	graduation of spraying equipment so that it applies the desired amount over a given area
Crusher	organisation specialising in crushing oilseeds to extract oil
Crown	the top part of the sugar beet's root from where the leaf stalks emerge
Cultural	without use of chemical pesticides
Chitting	potato growth (i.e. chits/sprouts) before planting
De-stoning	removing stones and clods from potato seed beds before planting and placing them in row bottoms where they will not interfere with tuber growth and harvesting
Dehydration	dried potato e.g. 'Smash'.
Desiccation	spray applied to crops literally to dry them out and therefore kill the crop
Double low	oilseed rape low in both undesirable erucic acid and glucosinolates
Drill	sow seed
Excess quota	the fine imposed by the P.M.B. for grwoing more than the allocated quota for that farm
F.E.P.A.	Food and Environmental Protection Act 1985
Fixed costs	costs which cannot readily be allocated to a specific enterprise on a farm, or will not vary with small changes in the scale/output of the enterprise

CONTACTS & TERMS

Forward contract	a sale of grain which is currently still being grown by the farmer, to his local merchant at an agreed price for delivery after harvest
Futures contract	this is the name for a forward contract to buy or sell a given amount and quality of grain / potatoes at an agreed time in the future and at an agreed price. This is done through London Fox
G.A.T.T.	General Agreement on Tariffs and Trade
Green top	potato crops harvetsed whilst foliage is still green and potatoes are immature
Guide Price	the EU Guide Price is set by the Council of Ministers at a level considered to be a fair return to the producers
Groundkeepers	sugar beet left on the farm, usually in the field, which goes on to complete its natural 2 year life cycle and shed seed
Growth regulator	a chemical altering crop growth patterns, especially for shortening and thickening stems in cereals to prevent lodging
Heavy land	soil with an above average clay content (difficult to work down to a seed bed with machinery)
High clearance sprayer	spraying equipment designed to work in tall crops without damaging plants
Host	a plant which acts as a home for a pest or disease
H.S.E.	Health and Safety Executive
Intervention	system of price support within the European Community based on buying surplus produce into store, so taking it off the market to maintain market price at a pre-agreed level
Leaching	soluble nitrates moving down through the soil profile, possibly into drainage water
Levy	the fee charged by the P.M.B. per hectare of crop grown
Lodge	crops bending over, making harvesting difficult
Lodging	the breaking of stems of cereals and grasses usually due to heavy rainfall and/or wind. This is often combined with high nitrogen uptake by the plant

CONTACTS & TERMS

Loam	a medium textured soil containing a balance of sand, clay and silt
Main crop	the greatest proportion of the UK crop grown to be stored in order to supply the market through the winter and spring until new potatoes are available
Malting	barley grown for brewing
Micro nutrients	elements required by plants in very small quantities
Micro-mole	unit of measurement for glucosinolate content
M.M.B.	Milk Marketing Board (now disbanded on 1st november 1994)) replaced by Milk Marque as just one of the milk marketing co-operatives in competition on the UK market
Mounted sprayer	sprayer, without wheels attached to the hydraulic lift of the tractor
Nitrogen index	an indication of residual nitrogen. This varies according to the previous crop
Oil seeds	a range of crops grown for the oil extracted from their seeds
Pesticides	any chemical which is used to kill, control or diminish not just insects but also weeds and diseases which challenge man, his crops, his domestic animals and his environment
pH	a measure of acidity or alkalinity. Range extends from zero to 14, pH 7.0 is neutral, below 7.0 is acidic.
Physiological age	an accurate method to determine the extent or degree of chitting in potatoes. Measured in unit of day C
P.M.B.	Potato Marketing Board
Polygonums	the Latin name for a particular family of spring germinating weeds
Pre-emergence	befiore the crop emerges
Post-emergence	after the crop emerges
Quota	the right to grow potatoes allocated on an area basis by the P.M.B.

Rotation	growing of a series of crops in regular order to avoid exhaustion of the soil and build up of diseases.
Seed treatment	chemicals applied to the seed before drilling often for crop protection purposes
Selective	choosing to affect certain parts only. For example a selective herbicide kilss weeds but leaves the crop relatively unaffected
Soil-acting residuals	substances remaining in the soil to act at a later date; for eaxample herbicides that remain in the soil to kill weeds as they germinate
Soil-moisture deficit	(SMD) the difference between soil water gain and soil water loss
Skin-set	potato skin test i.e. they can not easily be removed by the "thumb-nail test"
Spring crop	spring drilled crop
Spot price	term used for the actual price of grain offered for sale on the open market on any given day
Swathing	crop left out to mature
Tenant's capital	farm assets normally provided by tenants and includes livestock, machinery,crops in store, stocks, work in progress, cash and other assets needed to run a business
Threshold	a level or incidence of infestation of a disease which justifies the use of control measures such as pesticides
Tillers	shoots from the base of a stem of cereal plants
Trace elements	elements required in very small quantities by plants but which are essential for the normal metabolism of the plant
Tuber initiation	tuber formation
Uruguay Round	latest round of G.A.T.T. negotiations started in 1986 and due to finished in 1993
Variable costs	costs which can easily be allocated to a particular enterprise and vary directly with the scale/area of the crop grown - fertilizers, seed, sprays, casual labour, etc.
Varietal susceptibility	some varieties are susceptable to a particular herbicide product

CONTACTS & TERMS

Volunteers	plants grown by natural propogation rather than having been planted
Weed Beet	beet, usually the offspring of bolters or groundkeepers which become an annual weed and can carry over diseases from year to year
Wetter	added to pesticides or micronutrients to improve uptake through the foliage
Winter crop	autumn drilled crop
Working capital	assets required to finance the production cycle such as all variable cost items, plus labour, power costs, etc.